# BRIDGING THE AEGEAN

GROWING UP GREEK IN TURKEY

*Know thyself;*
*an unexamined life is not worth living.*
— Socrates

Copyright © 2015 Froso Hacipara Sendukas
All rights reserved.
ISBN: 1508567603
ISBN-13: 978-1508567608

# Acknowledgements

The seeds of this memoir were planted in the early 1990s when I was trying to come up with a creative project that I could share with friends at a "Blues" party.

My then partner, Lou, suggested that I write down some of the stories about my childhood in Turkey that I had been sharing with him. He even volunteered to type them for me.

Thus a project was born, that with time, took on more significance and became a long bur fruitful journey of mind and heart.

I had other helpers along the way. My granddaughter, Alexa, always showed an interest in what I wrote and gave me helpful feedback. Whenever I visited my son, Ronny, and his wife, Lisa, in California, they never failed to ask me to bring along some of my "stories" and were always eager to hear me read them.

My close friend, Connie, has been a loving listener of my childhood memories since the day we met, some 33 years ago.

My son, Perry, and daughter-in-law, Vanessa, have been totally supportive of this and all my other endeavors through the years and even helped me come up with the book title. I thank them from the bottom of my heart.

My son, Chris, who has tried valiantly to cure me of my technophobia answered all my "digital" questions.

When publishing started to become a reality, my editor, Sue Gaines, was a big help.

My lifelong friends, Uğur and Verdi Adam, have consistently shown me through the years that true friendship knows no boundaries.

They, and a parade of other supportive friends through the years, namely Betty, Pete and Dolly, as well as my old—but not forgotten—"Course of Miracles" group, have all influenced my life and my writing.

My gratitude goes to all of them.

# Dedication

For my wonderful grandchildren:

Alexa

Zach

Emily Anastasia

Natalie

Benjamin

Sammy

Peter

and to the memory of my mother, Anastasia Moshos who I know would be proud.

# Table of Contents

GROWING UP GREEK IN TURKEY ............... 1
THE ISLAND ............... 13
GREEN EYES ............... 33
NAME DAY ............... 41
MY MOTHER'S FAITH ............... 45
THE DAY I MET THE NEXT-TO-LAST KING OF GREECE ............... 55
FIRST DATE, FIRST LOVE ............... 61
THE ANEMIA SAGA ............... 69
THE VENDOUZES ............... 77
THE GIFT ............... 83
A GODLY MAN ............... 91
THE VULNERABILITY OF YOUTH ............... 113
THE SYMBOL OF VIRGINITY ............... 133
THE LAST TRIP ............... 145
BLACK SKIN ............... 151
THE TAXI DRIVER ............... 155
ANASTASIA AND DIMITRI ............... 163
MY MOTHER'S LOVE ............... 177
RETURN TO EPHESUS ............... 185
AN UNPLEASANT ENCOUNTER IN MARMARIS ............... 203
TAKING THE FERRY FROM TURKEY TO GREECE ............... 207

# BRIDGING THE AEGEAN

## GROWING UP GREEK IN TURKEY

For many years now, ever since I came to the United States, whenever I meet new people, we go through the same conversation scenario almost every time. They hear my foreign accent and immediately ask me where I'm from.

"I was born in Istanbul, Turkey," I say.

"Oh, so you are Turkish," they say.

"Actually, I'm more Greek than Turkish," is my response.

I see the puzzled look on their face, and I try to explain.

At the time I was growing up in Turkey ('40s and '50s), there was a large Greek minority—about 100,000—mostly living in Istanbul and surrounding areas. This minority population had a different religion (Greek Orthodox, Christian instead of Muslim); different language (modern Greek) spoken among themselves and at home; and some cultural differences.

Legally, there was no segregation in Turkey. After all, you could not really tell from appearance who was Greek in ethnic origin and who was Turkish. The charismatic founder of the modern Republic of Turkey (that replaced the Ottoman Empire), Mustafa Kemal Atatürk, had decreed in the 1920s that all Turks had to give up their religious-based clothing and dress in Western style clothes. No more long black robes and *çarşaf* (head scarf) for women, and no more *fez* (cone-shaped iconic red hat with black tassel) for men.

Atatürk told the country that the above decree—along with the enactment of new secular laws instead of the religious laws—was necessary to the modernization Turkey, enabling it to progress and compete in the Western world.

Even though Greeks and Turks were similar in appearance, in reality, they lived in two different societies and mostly stayed put within their own ethnic/social circles. The great gathering place for Greeks, aside from the Greek Orthodox Churches, was a community center called *Elinikos Siloyos* (the Hellenic Club). I remember the place well, my family and I spent a lot of time there. The club was always full of people. There would often be speakers on weekends discussing topical issues of the day of interest to the Greek population. There would also be festive social gatherings to celebrate Greek holidays, and once in a while, as a special treat, we would have visiting musicians and singers from Athens. And in typical Greek fashion, there was always food, no matter what the occasion. I remember as a child, while my parents were listening to some speaker or other, being bored with the proceedings and wandering to other meeting rooms in search of a favorite culinary treat like *spanako pita* (spinach pie) or *baklava* or *halva* (a sweet semolina pudding).

# BRIDGING THE AEGEAN

My parents did not object to my wandering around the place. This was a safe family center, and there were always other children around doing the same thing. Adults would watch us with an indulgent but firm eye, intent on keeping some kind of collective order in the place. They did not hesitate to correct us if we were too loud, or if our behavior stepped out of line, no matter whose children we were. Even though we lived in a big city and not in a village, we were all part of the same religious and cultural minority so, in a sense, we were everybody's children!

Then after I explain all of this, the typical question is, "But how was it *really* to grow up Greek in Turkey? Wasn't it tense and difficult? We've always heard that Greeks and Turks don't get along."

I smile and reply that, yes, the situation had its tense moments but it wasn't that bad. I cannot honestly say that I lived in fear or even a lot of distress growing up. I remember family members and their friends would complain about some unfair treatment, especially when it came to business matters and taxes, and would lament the fact that there were no Greeks representing them in local government. The truth is that I don't remember there ever being any Greek candidates for office. Either they were not interested, or more likely, they were not asked by the political parties to run. Being young, I didn't really care about politics. I was more interested in the fashions of the day or the latest hit song.

In general the atmosphere was relatively calm, at least through my childish and adolescent eyes. My mother admonished me at times to

## Froso Hacipara Sendukas

neither speak Greek loudly in the streets of Istanbul, nor to publicly display my cross pendant. A couple of times I failed to listen to these admonitions; I would then hear the word *gâvur* which means "infidel", whispered in my direction. Of course that was far from pleasant, but after a while I accepted the fact that I was living in a Muslim society and that displays of Christianity were not welcome or easily tolerated by some of its citizens.

The Greeks would console themselves about real or imagined incidents by privately telling each other that as an ethnic race, Greeks were superior to Turks. "Look at Istanbul's commerce—most of it is run by Greek merchants, and successful ones at that. They can't do without us," they would say, "Isn't that right? And after all, wasn't Istanbul Greek at one time?"

In fact, among Greeks, Istanbul was never called "Istanbul," it was always called "Constantinople", its Byzantine name. There were even some diehards who would talk seriously about Istanbul becoming Greek again one day and that they would go to the famous Byzantine church (now a museum), *Haghia Sophia*, to sing Greek hymns!

As a teenager I would laugh whenever I heard such remarks. A few of us would even criticize our elders about their attitudes and would tell ourselves that maybe the Greeks shared some of the blame for any ill treatment toward them by the Turks.

# BRIDGING THE AEGEAN

Then a fateful day arrived on September 6, 1955, and I was no longer laughing. I was twenty-one years old and had just finished my junior year at the American College for Girls. I was pining for my boyfriend who had just left Turkey a month earlier for the United States to finish his studies at the University of Texas. My biggest concern at the time was how to convince my mother to let me go to the United States the following year after my graduation to join my boyfriend and get married. Being her only, treasured child, this was no easy matter.

On that fateful day I was staying with my family on the island of Burgaz (*Antigoni* to Greeks), where I had spent many summers of my childhood. This beautiful island, off the coast of Istanbul, was a popular summer vacation place, especially for the Greeks of Istanbul who tended to congregate there, renting cottages for 2–3 months, enjoying the beauty of the island with its natural beaches. No cars were allowed on the island, people walked, rode a bike, or hired a donkey to take them where they wanted to go.

I will never forget that September morning for as long as I live! I woke up to a scene of great agitation and distress. I saw adults in my household and neighborhood either crying or huddling in small groups, sharing whispers of distress. When I asked what on Earth was going on, I was told that the previous night, while we were asleep, there had been some terrible riots in Istanbul. Windows of Greek-owned businesses were smashed and the shops were looted. Numerous Greek churches, some of them dating back to the Byzantine era, were burned to the ground. Damage, vandalism, and defacement had been inflicted on anything and everything that was known or identified as being owned by persons of Greek origin, most of them Turkish citizens.

Even the dead were not spared. There was considerable vandalism in Greek cemeteries; crosses were pulled or dug out of gravestones and thrown aside and dead bodies of some Greek patriarchs were unburied and profaned. There were even rumors that relics of saints were burned or thrown to wild dogs.

While all these horrific things were going on, the Police (according to onlookers) looked away and did nothing to stop the widespread carnage that lasted several hours, into the morning of September 7. There was strong suspicion, by the Greeks mostly, that the riots were organized and controlled by the government.

At the time it was hard to know what to believe. For days, weeks, and months following the riots, rumors were flying everywhere and spreading (as rumors tend to do) and I could tell, just from looking into familiar faces and talking with them, that Greek fears were escalating. Nobody really knew which rumors were true and which were not. Were the riots a one-time occurrence, or were there more coming? Would we ever truly feel safe again in the land where we lived, even on the idyllic island of Burgaz? It was hard not to feel helpless and hopeless.

People around me, with anxious faces, were whispering that none of the malignant craziness of the previous night made any sense. True, Greece

# BRIDGING THE AEGEAN

and Turkey were feuding over the island of Cyprus once again, but the Greeks of Turkey had nothing to do with this ongoing territorial fight; we were merely tense observers. Were the riots partly because of resentment over the strong Greek presence in local commerce? Or were they a violent knee-jerk retaliation to a current journalistic rumor (that later proved to be false) that the childhood home of the founder of modern Turkey, Atatürk, had been bombed in the Greek city of Thessaloniki? We didn't have any answers, just questions, suppositions and a flurry of wild rumors. All I knew was that for the first time in my life, I felt considerable fear about living in my place of birth.

I was also deeply worried about my father. I had been told by people who had already been to the city that his photography studio, located on one of the main streets of Istanbul, was one of the Greek-owned businesses that had been broken into and vandalized. My father was a well-known photographer, heavily patronized by both the Greek and the Turkish communities.

So it was with a great deal of apprehension that I boarded the 7:30 a.m. ferryboat the next morning to visit my father and see the damage for myself, despite my mother's concerns for my safety. The ferryboat, even though packed as usual with mostly Greek commuters, was strangely quiet that morning. You could practically feel the tension and gloom in the air. Whereas most mornings people were heard talking aloud and joking, or playing backgammon and card games, this morning all I saw was some secretive, furtive whispering and somber faces among the mostly male commuters. The sadness on the boat was palpable. I even saw some Greek men that I knew hiding their faces behind newspapers so no one would see them crying.

As the ferryboat started gliding along the beautiful blue-gray waters of the Marmara and Aegean Seas, I, who ordinarily loved ferryboat rides, on this morning did not have any eyes or appreciation for the beauty around me. I kept dreading what I was going to find once we reached Istanbul.

The ferryboat docked and I looked around not knowing what to expect. Everything looked normal around the dock, but then this wasn't a Greek business area. I took a taxi to Father's studio. The Turkish taxi driver was uncharacteristically quiet. As we were going toward our destination I could see the damage to many shops we were passing along the way, as well as the graffiti and vandalism.

My father's studio was on Beyoğlu (or *Pera*, as my fellow Greeks called it). It was and is one of the main streets in the city. My heart was beating fast as I got out of the taxi, I was afraid to look at the front of the studio. The glass window case in the front of the shop was my father's pride and joy; that's where he would position his favorite framed photographs of clients. A large framed picture of me had been placed in the center of the display. This morning, the glass display front was demolished, there was glass everywhere and photographs with broken frames were lying scattered all around. When I saw my crumpled picture on the floor behind the shattered glass, I started crying. As I went inside my father came to greet me with a hug and red eyes. "Did you see what they did to me?" he asked, and started sobbing. I did not know how to comfort him; all I could do was to hug him back and cry with him. It felt like all the Greeks of Turkey were crying right along with us! It was the end of our world as we knew it, and things would never be the same—ever again.

Thousands of Greeks holding Greek citizenship were expelled from Turkey within the next two years; my father was one of them. My mother, who had been born in Istanbul and was divorced from my father, remained in Istanbul till she died, saying, "This is my home, I'm not going anywhere." In September of 1956, exactly a year after the riots, having graduated from the American College for Girls, and having secured a scholarship to an American University, I left Turkey and came to the United States of America with my mother's full blessing. My mother, who had been so distressed about seeing her only child go so far away, suddenly changed her mind after the riots and told me she was glad to see me leave Turkey. She even managed a smile amidst her tears when she hugged me 'goodbye' at the airport. Years later I learned from family friends that the moment my plane took off and I was out of sight, Mother had fainted.

Soon after the riots, even Greeks holding Turkish citizenship started leaving Turkey and emigrating to Greece, Canada, and the United States, or anywhere else they had relatives or people they knew. Within the next ten years a mass exodus took place. Where there had been 80,000 Greeks by official count in Turkey (most of them in Istanbul) in 1955, there were only 40,000 in 1965, and the number continued to dwindle. When I went back home in 1980 for my mother's memorial service, my mother's friends told me that there were barely 8,000 Greeks left in Istanbul. The message had been heard in 1955 and understood: "Greeks are no longer welcome in Turkey." This had been our homeland for thousands of years; Greeks were the original natives of the country dating back to the Byzantine Empire. Suddenly we had to establish our roots elsewhere.

As "ethnic cleansings" go, this was, relatively speaking, rather "mild" except to the thousands of Greeks who lost their beautiful homeland and their hard-earned assets. Not a single shot was fired, and there were no concentration camps, though some Greeks were trampled and beaten when they tried to protect their property. At the time, there were no political consequences for Turkey, no international outcry, not even many articles written that I know of, except in Greek newspapers and a few global news magazines. Everything that had happened seemed to have been invisible to the rest of the world.

Years later I read in *Time* magazine that ex-Turkish Prime Minister Adnan Menderes, had been executed in Turkey for "crimes against the country," including inciting and organizing the 1955 anti-Greek riots! As I read the news item I felt I was being punched in the stomach.

# BRIDGING THE AEGEAN

For me, the facts tell only part of the story. The reality of what happened to the Greeks of Turkey hit me hardest in 1980 when I returned to Istanbul for my mother's memorial service. I visited a Greek church of my childhood that used to be packed every Sunday morning with families attending Greek Orthodox services. There were a total of five elderly ladies in the church, praying. I saw the almost empty church, remembered its former glory, and burst into tears.

Froso Hacipara Sendukas

# BRIDGING THE AEGEAN

## THE ISLAND

I wonder if young wives, all dressed up in pretty dresses, with their children in tow, still do the ritual promenade on warm summer evenings on the island of Burgaz (or *Antigoni* as I and my fellow Greeks called it).

This particular promenade, (*peripato* or *volta*), consisted of walking back and forth in a slow leisurely fashion along the seashore while waiting for the ferryboats to bring commuting husbands/fathers home from their daily jobs on the mainland, Istanbul.

During the 1940s and '50s, I was one of those children walking with my mother while waiting for my father to join us in the evening after he closed his photography studio, *Foto Şehir,* in Istanbul.

I remember the daily promenade as a social affair, with the women chatting as they walked, exchanging pleasantries and gossip as the ferryboats would start arriving, one every fifteen minutes or so, around 7:00 p.m. full of commuters. By 8:00 p.m. most of the commuters would have made it back to the island, and the crowd around the dock would be a lot thinner. Since my father was usually a late arrival, we had plenty of time for my mother to talk with her women friends, while I would walk or play nearby with my own friends. Occasionally vendors would mill around us in the street trying to lure hungry islanders like ourselves to try their wares—mostly steamed corn on the cob or strong

## Froso Hacipara Sendukas

Turkish coffee with a thick layer of foam on top carried on huge brass trays and brought outside to sidewalk tables in the small cafes that lined the dockside.

I was too young for coffee, but I adored steamed corn on the cob, so the moment I would hear "*mısır, mısır*" (corn, corn), I would beg my mother to let me have some. Mostly she would refuse my pleas saying it was too close to dinnertime and that the corn would spoil my appetite. All true statements, but I certainly didn't care. Occasionally, especially when my father was even later than usual, she would give in and I would savor the hot corn with salt as its only flavoring, tasting better than any corn I ever had or would ever have!

After some time, the commuters would disembark from the ferryboats and each family group would claim their returning *pater familias*. Almost all the commuters were men; there were very few women who worked outside the home at the time in Turkey unless they were very poor or extremely dedicated to the concept of having a career. After greeting and hugging their commuters, the families would depart for their summer cottages and the evening meal. Of course it would have been unthinkable for these families to eat before the "man of the house" came home. Thus would end the ritual promenade of summer evenings on the island of Burgaz.

I remember as a child feeling sorry for my father and the other commuting fathers, thinking that they were missing so much of island

## BRIDGING THE AEGEAN

life by being in the city all day and only joining their families for evenings and weekends. Looking back now as an adult, as well as a practicing psychotherapist, I think I was missing the point. Most of the men were probably happy to be providing a long vacation for their families (the usual island stay was three and a half months, June–September). They did not have to be rich to accomplish this, either. The island cottages were so reasonably priced at the time that most middle-class families could afford to rent them for the whole summer. Burgaz was by far the island of choice for most Greeks of Istanbul, and since Greeks were at the time the leading merchants of the city, it was well within their means to spend summers there.

Another reason, I now realize, that I did not need to feel sorry for them back then, was that the commuting men were able to relax after work in various ways for the hour or so that it took for the ferryboats to travel the distance from Istanbul to Burgaz. They could converse with their fellow commuters, some of them friends or neighbors, or read the newspaper, or play cards and games, especially the popular backgammon, *tavli*, while having tea or coffee, or a beer. The few times I spent the day in the city with my mother, later joining my father on the commuter boats, I remember hearing loud and lively backgammon games all over the interior of the boat and on the outside decks. Since no cars were allowed on any of the islands, these large boats were designed for passengers only.

## Froso Hacipara Sendukas

In case the commuters didn't feel like reading or conversing or playing games, there was also the opportunity to sit in the quieter corners of the boat by a window and watch the lovely colors of the Sea of Marmara graduating from blue to deeper cobalt blue, or gray on rainy days, and maybe drift into a little nap until awakened by the conductor yelling, "Burgaz, Burgaz!" Certainly not a bad way to relax before joining the family for the evening ahead.

After dinner, another type of ritual promenade would take place on the island. This would be the evening peripato and it would usually take place between 8:30 p.m. and 10:00 p.m. on a street at the edge of the seashore. This time around, the crowd tended to be less family oriented, younger and more lively. There would be a steady stream of strollers walking arm-in-arm with their own friends, young men as well as women. Flirting with meaningful glances or exchanging playful teasing remarks as they passed each other—all under the watchful eyes of their parents and elders walking more sedately, but never too far from their youngsters, especially their daughters.

In my teenage years, this was my favorite type of promenade. The island streets close to the water would be dimly lit, and since there were no barriers between the street level and the sea, most of the light would come from the moon reflected on the surface of the water. On summer evenings when there was a full moon, these evening walks would be magical. I know that nostalgia probably colors my memory of these

# BRIDGING THE AEGEAN

walks, but I do remember them as a lovely way to pass a summer evening, with nature providing most of the entertainment.

Oh, how I loved those summers of my youth spent in Burgaz, even while I took the simple and natural beauty of the island for granted and did not really appreciate the opportunity to spend a whole summer there with a lot of outdoor time instead of being cooped up in a small city apartment like I was the rest of the year. I knew that one of my closest friends, Vera, did not spend her summers on the island or other resort, probably because her parents could not afford to rent a summer place. But at the time I naively assumed that everybody all over the world had long summer vacations if they chose to.

I knew as a child that even when money was rather tight my mother would make sure to save some money during the year so we could afford to rent an island cottage for the summer months. As summer approached, my father would sometimes say, especially in the early years of owning his studio, that he did not know how he could afford a long vacation. My heart would sink when I would hear him talk about tight finances. Then I would hear my mother say, "We have to do this for Frosula; she needs the sunshine and the outdoors, and the ocean is the best tranquilizer in the world," and my stomach would settle down, knowing that my mother would somehow make it happen and we would be back in Burgaz some time in early June.

## Froso Hacipara Sendukas

It is true that the atmosphere of the island was conducive to lots of relaxation. There were no cars, buses, trolleys, or any mechanized transport allowed on the Prince Islands, of which Burgaz was one. There were three main islands: *Kınalıada, Heybeliada,* and *Büyükada,* or their Greek names: *Proti, Halki,* and *Pringipo.* The biggest island of the four was Büyükada, Turkish for "big island." Not only is this island the biggest of them all but objectively speaking, it's also the most beautiful, with gorgeous cliff-top views of the Sea of Marmara where the wealthy have purchased lovely villas on the edge of the cliffs. Because of its considerable size there are numerous rows of horse-drawn carriages in the main square of the island, close to the docks, waiting for weary commuters to hire them to take them home, or for island visitors there for the day to take a tour of the island. Büyükada in the 1940s and 1950s was like a microcosm of Istanbul; most of the year-round and summer residents were Muslim Turks with a sprinkling of other ethnic minorities like Greeks, Armenians, and Jews, with a few Italians thrown in for good measure. However, most Greeks who could afford to rent or buy second homes would still choose Burgaz, known informally as the "Greek" island. The Armenian population would flock to the second island, Kınalıada. The Jews of Istanbul, numerically not as large a population as the Greeks or Armenians, could be found on all the islands. And, according to my mother, the Jewish women were noticeable for their flair and elegant dress.

Burgaz, being a smaller island, did not have horse-drawn carriages in the main square or anywhere else for that matter. Since there were no hotels on Burgaz, we did not have many tourists. Once in a while, one would see a slow elderly mule carrying an older islander, but other than that there was no transportation except for bicycles or where our feet would take us. That made for a quiet island with no traffic, pollution or the visiting throngs of the Big Island. Crime was virtually unknown, except for a petty robbery here and there. The only noise besides that of playing children would be the occasional wailing of Turkish music coming from a radio played loudly inside a house or restaurant, and the call to prayers that came five times each day from the *muezzin* of the local mosque. We, the Greeks of the island, however, took pride in the fact that it was the dome of a Greek church that overlooked the harbor. I looked forward every summer to the feast day of Saint Efrosini in that same church, September 25th, which is my name day (my baptismal name was Efrosini, though I was always called Froso like all the other Greek girls of the same name). It made my mother proud that one summer I was asked to hand out candles to parishioners as they entered the church on that special day.

I remember as a teenager complaining to my friends that island life was boring and there was nothing to do but swim in the sea every day and walk along the seashore! There was no television in the early 1950s in Turkey, so the only commercial entertainment was listening to the radio, and since almost all music played on local stations was traditional Turkish folk music, I did not care for that either. My friends and I were dying to hear American pop music like the songs we would occasionally hear in foreign movies or on records brought in by individuals who had traveled to Europe or the United States. As I got older another entertainment emerged in Burgaz. We suddenly had a new outdoor movie theater that would, on certain summer weekends, play old European and American movies, unmercifully and painfully dubbed into Turkish or with confusing subtitles that were not even remotely related to what was happening on the screen. (Looking back now I'm guessing that Turkish governmental censors, famous for their heavy-handed approach, played a strong part in this and probably cut out whatever seemed offensive to Turkish morals and/or the Moslem religion.) The visible gaps in the foreign movies shown would make us all laugh or sigh with frustration because we would notice that any and all kissing scenes were either cut or abruptly terminated. We wanted to see what was going on, and instead we would get either a blank screen or a segue to another scene. It would make us all groan!

The movies were shown inside a makeshift canvas tent. If the night was cloudy, my girlfriends and I would go early to the tent so we could sit up front on plastic chairs or on the benches in the middle. We knew from unpleasant experience that if we sat towards the back of the tent or too close to the tent poles, and it rained, we would get drenched.
And, of course, with the movie theater being outdoors, if there were heavy rain, thunder and lightning, they would stop showing the movie. We would all groan again.

Life continued on the island every summer in its relaxed easy-going lifestyle. Even my parents' divorce when I was twelve years old and their

# BRIDGING THE AEGEAN

subsequent marriages to other people did not alter the pattern for long. My mother and new stepfather did take me to another resort for a few summers after their marriage, a village called *Yeşilköy* (green village). That seemed to be my stepfather's choice. Yeşilköy was about thirty-five minutes from Istanbul, and could only be reached by train or car. As its name indicated, it had a lot of trees and was a very pleasant resort town full of restored Victorian houses and even some antique shops. At first I was not too happy about the change of summer venues; I missed Burgaz, but I quickly adapted to the change, especially because my best friend, Melina, spent her summers there also. Her family owned a large second home there equipped with a charming gazebo, volleyball court and tennis court. It had it all. The gazebo had comfortable rattan chairs and two hammocks. Melina and I would lie for hours on these hammocks, talking about anything and everything that touched our young teenage lives.

Melina's father was a wealthy man, he owned a factory near Yeşilköy. The lot where their house and my beloved gazebo stood were so large that one could build at least two other houses on it. On weekends we would often have lively volley ball games with family members and friends joining us. The only one who refused to join us was Melina's mother, a rather sour looking woman who would complain at times that we were too noisy on the court and were giving her a headache. That would be a signal to Melina's father to leave our company and go inside the house to attend to his wife, albeit reluctantly. Melina was my best friend through elementary school, junior high, high school, and college. Even though we went to different schools after sixth grade, somehow we managed to stay close through the years despite the fact, as in most Turkish homes at the time, there was no telephone at my house, and certainly no family car.

In the summertime I would bicycle to her house every morning and spend practically all day with her. Occasionally, as the days grew warmer in July and August, we would beg her parents to let us take their boat out to the Sea of Marmara that was close by. When they would acquiesce, they would call the "kapitan" (captain) as we all called him, and the kindly middle-aged gentleman would take the helm of the boat and take us for a long boat ride. Whenever we would see clear turquoise water, we (Melina, her younger sister, Tina, Tina's friend and I) would shout at the kapitan to stop the boat; he would oblige us by dropping anchor and we would dive off the boat and swim till we got too tired to move. I remember one particular day when the water was so clear and beautiful we stayed out longer than usual. By the time we came back to the harbor, Melina said she was not feeling well. She was red in the face and had a hard time riding her bicycle to her home even though it was a short distance from where the boat was docked. When we arrived at her house, she was violently ill and throwing up all over the place. Her mother, while calling the doctor, started yelling at our group saying we should have known better than to stay out in the sun for so long. Melina and I were all of fourteen at the time; Tina and her friend were about twelve years old. Her mother continued for a while to harangue us saying she was going to stop the boat rides once and for all. I wanted to run home; I didn't like the yelling and I thought we got unfairly blamed, but I stayed for a while and waited for the doctor because I was worried about Melina's health. The doctor said it was sunstroke and that she would be OK in a few days, which she was. I went to visit her the next day and privately told her what her mother had said. I didn't mention the yelling but Melina remembered bits and pieces that she had overheard. She said for me not to take to heart what her mother said, she had her moods after all, and Melina assured me she would talk to her father about continuing the boat rides. "I'm sure it will be all right, Froso, Dad hardly ever refuses me when I ask for a favor, don't worry."

I heard her and wanted to believe her, but remembering her mother's scolding and yelling, I refrained from bicycling over to Melina's for a few days. Then one day, a week later, there came my friend, looking healthy and fit, riding her bicycle to my family's rented cottage and asking me why I had not been to see her. "I missed you," she said, "Where have you been?" So we went back to our routine and my favorite activity of sitting in her gazebo having our endless talks, or occasionally both of us reading books, with a glass of lemonade by our side. I would confide in her my distress about my parents' divorce and what a big scandal it had become in the Greek community. She would try to comfort me and tell me that a lot of families had secrets and not to mind the stares of strangers. Once in a while we would overhear her parents having an argument in the house and we would retreat even further into the quiet peacefulness of the gazebo.

## Froso Hacipara Sendukas

In later years, after Melina's father died from a heart attack, her statement about secrets in families would turn out to be quite prophetic. That's when my friend became embroiled in a family scandal of her own, much bigger than mine. We learned that her father was never legally married to her mother. His original wife who could not bear children, refused to give him a divorce, so he lived with Melina's mother and had two children with her. He also supported her two children from her previous marriage. He did all this while also supporting his legal wife with the condition that she would keep their secret. After Melina's father died, the legal wife, not feeling the need to be silent any more, emerged from the shadows, claiming that she was entitled to all his money and possessions. The only property that escaped her was the house with the beautiful gazebo in the resort town of Yeşilköy because he had placed it in Melina and Tina's names.

Poor Melina! Not only was she grieving the loss of her father, definitely her favorite parent, but she also had to face all the repercussions of a big ugly scandal in the Greek community. From being respected as leaders in the community, her family was shunned practically overnight. I tried to comfort her in her grief and distress, but the world was, for my friend, an overwhelming place for a while. She told me that neither she nor her sister had any knowledge of her father's marital situation and so they were shocked and dismayed. She was, like me, only eighteen years old at the time. She now had to mature quickly and comfort her younger sister. She also had to become the head of the family because her mother, devastated by her husband's sudden death, as well as the loss of favor in the community, became quite distraught and incapable of making any decisions. Eventually the family had to sell their beautiful resort home to make ends meet. I cried with Melina about its loss and about the emotional and financial devastation that she and her family were experiencing. After all this it was very hard for me to face Yeşilköy without my best friend, and I convinced my mother (and she in turn convinced my stepfather) to return to the island of Burgaz for our future summer vacations.

I was nineteen years old and in my first year in the American College for Girls when one summer night, a committee made up of two Greek Islanders and one Armenian lady came to our house to talk my parents, and then me, about allowing me to participate in the Miss Burgaz contest, taking place the following weekend. This was to be a small part of the bigger contest, Miss Adalar (of all the islands), and that could lead to participation in the Miss Istanbul contest, and finally, Miss Turkey. My mother said that she was flattered on my behalf but hesitant. She took me aside and asked me privately if I wanted to do this. She added that the Greeks of the island were especially keen on my representing them and it was surely an honor, but I didn't have to do any of this if I didn't want to. She concluded by saying that being a member of a non-Muslim minority I would probably not win anyway. I asked my stepfather who, in my estimation, was an intelligent and wise man and whose advice I respected, what he thought of the idea. He said, "Well, it might be an interesting experience to participate in a small beauty pageant like this one, as long as you don't take the results too seriously." I thought, "Why not?" It would only take a few minutes of my time and I could laugh about it with my girlfriends later and maybe even brag a little.

The next few days seemed to endlessly drag on. It was hard to fall asleep at night. I kept rehearsing in my mind what I would say if I won or lost. I wanted to make an impression as a gracious loser. I asked my mother what I should wear to the beauty contest. She in turn called the committeewoman who had come to our house and asked her the same question. My mother reported to me that the lady (whose name I do not recall) replied that I could wear whatever I wanted, nothing too fancy.

This was no Miss America Pageant. There were no swimsuit, evening gown, or even talent divisions. I and the other contestants would introduce ourselves, walk around the dance floor of the restaurant/club where the contest was to take place and then the judges would ask us each a question about our special interests and that would be it. I was very glad about the choice of setting for the event. This particular restaurant was owned by an Armenian family and was a favorite of my mother and my stepfather, so I was quite familiar with it. The committee probably chose it because it was the biggest restaurant on the island and actually the only one with a dance floor. I can still see in front of my eyes Madame Stella, the no-nonsense matriarch of the clan and the owner-chef of the restaurant. She was a tall, big-boned lady with gray hair always pulled back in a severe bun, and she ran the restaurant with a firm hand and soft heart. We, the young people of the island knew that if we went to her restaurant when hungry, she would feed us even if we didn't have enough money to pay the total bill. She would shrug her massive shoulders and scold us about coming to her place without enough cash and then send us plates of food from the kitchen anyway, while shouting at us at the same time. Delicious food, at that! There were only a handful of restaurants in the island, but her cooking was by far the best. I still salivate remembering her eggplant and zucchini patties, her most famous specialty.

So that's where the contest took place on a balmy Saturday evening, in July of 1953. My mother and I had decided that I would wear a simple black cotton skirt with a sleeveless silk pink blouse. I wore medium-heeled black pumps to complete the outfit. The contest was to take place at 8:30 p.m. My mother, stepfather and I walked into the restaurant at around 8:00 p.m. to find almost all the tables full and some excited looking young girls (fellow contestants, I assumed) milling around the dance floor, chatting with each other. I noticed to my dismay that a couple of them wore evening gowns, but the rest were dressed more casually like I was. I looked around, saw the crowd, realized how pretty some of the contestants were, and I wondered what possessed me to put myself on the line tonight. There were six judges seated at a long table on one side of the dance floor and I tried not to look in their direction so as not to become even more nervous that I already was.

## Froso Hacipara Sendukas

The Mayor of Burgaz gave a little speech reminding the judges and the restaurant crowd that even though tonight's contest was small they needed to remember that it was part of a much bigger cycle of beauty pageants and thus very important. Whoever was selected Miss Burgaz would compete in a month's time with the winners of the other islands for the title of Miss Prince Islands (*Adalar Güzeli*) and that winner in turn would automatically be qualified to compete in the Miss Istanbul contest. Who knows, maybe even the Miss Turkey contest beckoned tonight's winner and eventually Miss Europe and even Miss World! At other times, in other places, hearing our pompous Mayor describe all these possibilities about potential world fame for our small island of Burgaz would have made me laugh. On this July evening, however, nervously standing on a dance floor surrounded by other nervous young women, the speech made my head swim. Once more that evening, I thought to myself, "What have I gotten myself into?" I calmed myself with the thought that being Greek, I didn't have much of a chance to go down the line or even get in on the bottom rung of this fame ladder. "All I have to do is parade around the dance floor a couple of times and then go home," I thought.

I made myself smile and walked around with the other girls, trying to stay away from the evening gown-clad ones. I had a lot of mixed feelings; I was somewhat nervous, somewhat excited, somewhat self-conscious, wanting the experience to be over soon. The next thing I remember is one of the judges asking me why I was going to college (in 1953 few young women in Turkey went to colleges or universities). I replied that I had always wanted to have a vocation that would allow me to help orphaned children get adopted and that a higher education would make this goal more possible. A little while later a bouquet of red roses was thrust into my hands and a red and gold silk banner was placed across my chest that said in glittery letters "Burgaz Güzeli" (Miss Burgaz). I was astonished and elated at the same time. I looked at the table where my mother and stepfather sat and saw them looking at me with proud, loving eyes as they joined the crowd's applause. I was happy to be sharing this moment with them. My mother whispered, when I rushed to hug her, "Didn't I always tell you that you were the prettiest girl in the island?" I whispered back, "But you told me that I didn't have much of a chance tonight." She quickly replied, "I didn't want you to get crushed with disappointment in case you didn't win."

I didn't sleep much that night. I was too excited. I was nineteen years old and this was the biggest thing that had ever happened to me. Then morning came and reality started setting in. By mid-morning the whole island knew who had won the beauty contest the night before, even though there were very few phones in the island. Two of my girlfriends came to the house to congratulate me. Soon after complementing me, my friends chided me for keeping the news from them that I had been asked to enter the contest. Later, some of my mother's girlfriends started coming to the house and I overheard snippets of conversation to the effect that "good Greek girls" didn't really do things like that, e.g., enter beauty pageants. I saw my mother's face cloud with dismay and I was filled with anger that her friends were spoiling the joy of the previous evening. I didn't know then that the worst aftermath of the contest was yet to come. I had a prearranged date with my boyfriend that afternoon. He was my first serious boyfriend and I wondered how to break the news to him about the previous night and my new title. Knowing how reserved and private a person he was, I suspected he was not going to be happy about the news.

As I went to the harbor to wait for the ferryboat carrying him from Istanbul, I rehearsed lots of opening sentences in my head. What a waste of time and energy! Without even greeting me, the first words out of his mouth were, "What on earth possessed you to enter a beauty contest?" I was astounded that he already knew. I had forgotten how super fast the Greek community's "gossip express" worked. No telegraph office could match its speed. It was clear that somebody had communicated the news to my boyfriend, either in Istanbul or on the ferryboat. Before I had a chance to reply, he went on to say in a heated voice, "Don't you know the kind of society element that's involved in this contest? My parents were appalled when they heard that you won the island beauty contest. Let's hope that this was just an impulsive mistake on your part and that you are going to resign right away and let the contest runner-up go to the Miss Prince Islands extravaganza next month!" My heart sank at his words and all the joy and excitement of the night before faded and became tainted. My new title suddenly felt almost shameful and dirty. I protested feebly at his reproach, "Don't I even get congratulated about winning the contest?" I said. "No, you don't." was the cold reply, "The sooner we forget about this unfortunate incident, the better."

So I tried to do as he said and forget the contest. In my defense all I can say is that I was seriously in love for the first time in my life and hoped to marry the fellow. Even though a small voice inside me said that it was not OK for him to be such a killjoy when I was so happy, I refused to listen to that voice and attributed his reaction to jealousy and the influence of narrow-minded Greek thinking.

I told my mother that night that after giving the matter careful thought, I had decided to resign as Miss Burgaz. She said she understood and did not ask any probing questions. Being a wise woman and knowing local Greek mores, I'm sure she guessed at what had happened, even though I had not mentioned my boyfriend or his remarks. The negative comments of some of her friends had shaken her already. I wrote a letter of regret to the organizers of the beauty pageant, and that was that! A couple of weeks later, I read a column in our small island newspaper scolding me for resigning my title of Miss Burgaz and coyly suggesting that the readers of the newspaper would thus be deprived of the chance to admire my "big, expressive brown eyes"! I was in a commuter ferryboat as I read the article. I looked around me, feeling self-conscious and both flattered and embarrassed at the same time. I immediately put on my sunglasses, even though it was twilight, and rather dark inside the ferryboat, so that nobody would recognize me. "The perils of fame!" I thought, and then laughed at myself for taking the article so seriously.

## Froso Hacipara Sendukas

I did, however, feel somewhat irresponsible for quitting, and even for entering the contest in the first place. The runner-up did not win the Adalar Guzeli (Miss Prince Islands) contest, so her reign was very short. For a few months after these events, I would have occasional dreams relating to the contest and I would wake up feeling cowardly for not completing the cycle and giving in to my boyfriend's objections out of fear of losing him.

I'm in my sixties now and I still have the silk red and gold banner that says "Burgaz Güzeli," it's in the bottom of a rattan trunk. It traveled with me from Istanbul, Turkey to Baton Rouge, Louisiana to Alexandria, Louisiana to Baltimore, Maryland and finally to Houston, Texas. I'll show it to my grandchildren one day tell them that, even though in the long run character and integrity are more important than one's appearance, that it was still a magical moment to be a Greek nineteen-year-old and chosen "Miss Burgaz" that balmy summer evening on a small Turkish island.

# BRIDGING THE AEGEAN

## GREEN EYES

I was fifteen years old when I first saw him. He had curly black hair and green eyes, and I thought he was the most beautiful human being that I had ever set my eyes on. I don't remember his name but I do remember that I asked about him—discreetly, of course—and found out to my dismay that despite the color of his eyes, (unusual in a Turk) he was Turkish and a Muslim (as almost all Turks are).

I'll call him Erol. He was definitely not a young man that a Greek Orthodox girl like me should have been interested in. But when you're fifteen and your insides melt every time you see someone, who cares about religion and society's conventions?

This particular summer, when Erol came into my life, my family and I were renting a house in Yeşilköy, a coastal resort town about an hour away, by train, from Istanbul. The name of the town literally means "green village" and it is truly so. It was, at the time, a charming little town full of Victorian and Ottoman-era houses and numerous lush, green parks overlooking the Sea of Marmara. Fifty years ago it was a popular resort for many middle-class Greek, Turkish, Armenian and Jewish Istanbulites who liked to spend the summer in the gentle rolling hills of Yeşilköy to get away from the hectic urban atmosphere of the city. Some residents lived there year-round.

My closest childhood friend, Melina, spent all her summers in Yeşilköy. Her family—who was quite wealthy—didn't just rent a cottage, they owned a very large and lovely second home. Her father owned a factory close to the town. Consequently, she and I spent a lot of time in her home, especially in the backyard gazebo. That's where we were one day, both of us lying contentedly in two side-by-side hammocks, alternately reading our books and talking. At one point I excitedly told Melina that I kept seeing a certain young man around town and that he and I were exchanging shy but meaningful glances. I said, "I really think he likes me and he has the most gorgeous green eyes!" After listening for a while to my bubbly talk, she asked, "Is he Greek?" I hesitantly told her that I heard from some friends that he was Turkish and that his name was Erol. My usually mild mannered friend almost fell from her hammock and shouted, "Froso, have you gone nuts? Don't even think of meeting him somewhere or starting something! For one thing, you do know that our Greek families don't even believe in dating, especially for fifteen-year-olds. Have you forgotten how they want us to have chaperones, even when we're engaged to be married? And a Turk? Forget it. He is totally off limits to you."

I couldn't believe that my gentle friend, Melina, was saying all this. Not that it wasn't all true, it was, but I certainly didn't want to hear what she was saying. All I wanted was to keep daydreaming about Erol and his green eyes. In a huff, I hurriedly said goodbye and ran out of the gazebo. However, deep inside I knew that my friend was generally a mature and wise young woman, so her words shook me up. On my way home that afternoon on my bicycle (my most frequent mode of transportation in Yeşilköy), I started questioning my attraction to "my young man" and came down somewhat from the cloud I had been on. The inner reflection and curbing of my enthusiasm lasted about a week. Next thing I knew, I started noticing Erol slowly walking by my house on several occasions. I didn't think it was a coincidence. I must not have been the only one in town making inquiries. Somehow he must have found out where I lived. He would slowly walk by, whistling and looking up at my upstairs bedroom window. That's all I needed to get my romantic pulse racing again. I thought, "To heck with Melina's admonitions; he must really like me, why else would he walk by so frequently?"

That's how our own little private ritual started. As he walked by, I would look down to the street oh so casually, smile at him and then run to the family record player to play a romantic hit of the day. I had labeled it, "Our Song." The truth was that we had never even spoken to each other—not one word.

As I smiled at him and played the song, I fantasized a mile a minute. I thought I was being very subtle and not letting my mother suspect that anything out of the ordinary was going on. My mother, who was a pretty observant woman and no dummy, figured it out by the second week. All said to me was, "Do you have to have that record player on so loud, Frosula? The neighbors are starting to complain." She added, "That handsome young man who walks by our house so many times a day, he's Turkish, isn't he ? Be careful." I must have blushed something fierce, I could feel my face getting hot, and I must have turned red. I mumbled something to the effect that I didn't know what she was talking about, she just smiled and walked away.

Her comments gave me pause. I remember thinking that my mother was the least prejudiced person that I knew. She liked people based on their character, not their ethnicity or religion, and even though she was a faithful Greek Orthodox woman, she also held to the firm belief that any church, or temple, or mosque that worshipped God was a holy place for her. So I was startled to hear her tell me to be careful because she had guessed that Erol was a Turk. I told myself that I either had to forget him or not be so obvious. There was a serious taboo in both the Greek and Turkish communities against such attractions. I had often heard the gossip in the Greek community about the very few Greek/Turkish couples that defied convention and religion. These couples were shunned by both communities. Even their own families would not usually recognize these unions. They either had to leave Turkey or else live like pariahs in their own land. I met a young woman once who was in such a marriage; my only feeling at the time was immense pity for her. With these thoughts and preconceived notions, it's a wonder that I even allowed myself to feel attraction for that young man. It might be an indication of all the prohibitions of the time that I don't even recall his real name.

We met in person only once, Erol and I, during the annual fair that took place every August in Yeşilköy, right before the end of the summer season. It was a balmy summer evening with breezes from the Sea of Marmara mixed with the fragrant scents from the park where the fair was being held. I had gotten permission from my parents to attend with two girlfriends, with the provision that I had to return home by 10:00 p.m. I was lamenting the fact that Melina—who had stricter parents than the rest of us—had not been allowed to join us, when I spotted Erol standing by a roasted corn vendor's kiosk, looking at me. My heart skipped a beat, and I stopped dead in my tracks. One of my two girlfriends, in whom I had confided my semi-secret crush, but who did not know what Erol looked like said, "What's going on with you, Froso? Why aren't you walking? Oh, my God, Is that your young man over there? He's certainly looking at us intensely." I excitedly whispered to her that he was the one. "Well, he's certainly cute, look at those eyes!" I told her to be quiet, and not knowing what to do, asked my friends to walk in another direction. For quite a while Erol and I kept circling each other without talking or even approaching each other. We would just look at each other and then quickly look away.

I don't remember much of what my friends and I did that evening at the fair. I'm pretty sure we ate lots of cotton candy, that I loved, and rode the big noisy roller coaster. I have never liked roller coasters; they always make me somewhat nervous and leave me with a funny feeling in the pit of my stomach, especially when they swoop down. That night at the fair my head was so full of Erol and his green eyes that I rode the dreaded roller coaster like a robot, with hardly any reaction at all. I even forgot to eat a roasted ear of corn, one of my very favorite things to do at the fair.

Later, as my friends and I were looking at some multicolored scarves at another kiosk, I looked around and could not spot him anymore. I felt the stab of disappointment, thinking he must have left the fair and gone home. Just then, I felt a light pressure on my arm and then realized that a folded sheet of paper had been slipped into my hand. I turned around quickly but did not see anyone. I looked at the piece of paper. It was a poem written in Turkish. The title was "To The Most Beautiful Brown Eyes," I burst out laughing with pleasure. I had no doubt who the poem's author was. It seemed that all the time I was admiring his beautiful green eyes, he in turn was admiring my brown ones! At little while later, our paths crossed again, and taking my courage in hand, I thanked him in Turkish for the poem. He smiled and whispered, "Can we talk for a few minutes? I can meet you behind the roller coaster concession stand in five minutes." I excitedly told my girlfriends where I was going and why. "People will see you together and talk," they said, "You know how Greeks gossip, be careful and don't stay away too long. We will wait for you nearby." I was so excited and happy, I could hardly answer them. I had anticipated in fantasy this encounter for two months. Who cared about being careful!

I went flying around to the concession stand. Erol was waiting for me. He thanked me for coming and then told me he liked me a lot and thought about me all the time. I muttered something to the effect that he didn't even know me. I'll never forget his reply, "I look inside your eyes," he said, "and I know you." My heart melted on the spot. I thought that was so beautiful and so romantic I could hardly breathe. We then saw a group of people coming toward us in the semi-dark. He quickly leaned down to kiss me. I was so surprised that I moved my head and his kiss landed on my cheek close to my right ear. He then quickly walked away, and I stood there for quite a while touching my cheek in wonder, not wanting to end the moment and the spell.

My friends found me there in the same spot some time later. "We were worried about you, you stayed away far too long. It's close to our curfew time and we need to get back home. What on Earth happened? Did you talk to your admirer?" "Yes, yes, yes," I said, and I gave them an edited version of what had happened. "Oh, my God," they said, "That's so exciting, but wait a minute. Isn't he a Turk?"

I never saw Erol again. Even the strolling by my house stopped. I was devastated. A week later, I found out that Erol's father had suddenly gotten very ill and he and his family left Yeşilköy in a hurry to return to Istanbul. We had not exchanged either last names or addresses in Istanbul. I thought of him for some time and had numerous dreams for months about our one and only encounter. I had a fleeting hope of meeting him by chance in Istanbul, but that magical meeting never happened.

I was remembering that innocent flirtation of many years ago when I saw a story one day in our local paper in Houston, Texas about a couple

## Froso Hacipara Sendukas

in Bosnia. This was a true story that happened during the Bosnian-Serbian War in the former Yugoslavia. The young man was a Serbian Catholic and the young woman was a Bosnian Muslim. The names of the couple were Bosko and Admira. They were in love and wanted to marry and live a normal life in Belgrade. Their war-torn lands would not allow such a union. In desperation they decided to escape besieged Sarajevo and made a mad dash together behind a parliament building. Thirty yards from safety, a machine gunner killed Bosko. Admira was wounded; she crawled over and cradled him in her arms, and then she also died. For six days they lay together in a silent, frozen embrace. The area where they fell was covered and attacked constantly by snipers from both sides. A week later, some Serbs ventured out to recover the bodies of the young lovers.

Who killed them is a mystery. Each side blamed the other. "Bosko's mother", said the article, "does not know who is responsible and she is not trying to find out." She blames only a brutal endless war and a religious hatred that divides people who love each other and want to be together. Bosko's mother had knitted a sweater to place in their joint grave. I still get tearful whenever I think of that tragic couple.

Although there was no actual war in Turkey when I was growing up, I can't help but feel some sorrow about the generational enmity between Greeks and Turks that prevented Erol and I from ever finding out if we were meant to share more than a poem, and a kiss on the cheek.

# BRIDGING THE AEGEAN

## NAME DAY

The Greek community of Istanbul, or Constantinople, (as the Greeks have always called it), loves its traditional customs and celebrations. One of the most cherished was the annual Name Day Celebration.

It didn't matter whether you were young or old, wealthy or poor, you knew that lots of people were bound to come to your house on your Name Day every year. The Name Day was the Church Feast Day assigned to the Greek Orthodox saint whose name one took when baptized. My baptismal name is Efrosini. My grandmother always said that I was named for a saint she admired; and my mother would add that it didn't hurt that the name Efrosini also meant 'a mythological handmaiden to the goddess, Aphrodite, the goddess of love.' The only thing I ever really liked about my name is that it means 'joy' in ancient Greek.

No invitations were needed or even expected for this annual visit. Family friends and acquaintances would assume that they were welcomed to pay a visit—and expect a little nourishment as well. The nourishment would vary according to one's finances. It could be as little as a spoon of homemade preserves with a glass of water on the side, or as elaborate as a lavish buffet.

The only way to get out of these annual visitations would be to put a notice in the local Greek paper, saying that your were not able to observe your Name Day this year. Naturally there had to be a good reason for this. If you wanted your reputation in the community to remain decent, the most acceptable excuse for not receiving visitors was a recent death in the family. The only other excuse that would be tolerated was a serious illness—but that had to be a real illness and not a manufactured one. The illness did not have to be spelled out; the gossip mills being very strong in the Greek community, everybody knew what everybody had anyway.

There was a time during my teenage years when I found myself telling my mother that this annual Greek custom of uninvited guests descending upon one's doorstep was ridiculous, and I announced dramatically that I was not planning to stay home on my Name Day that year. Mother told me that this would be rude behavior, but if I really wanted to stay out of the house on St. Efrosini's Feast Day, come September 25$^{th}$, that I would be free to do so. "You will miss the celebration", she said, "I think that you will regret this." "Nonsense", I said, "It's mostly your friends who come over on that day anyway, mother; I have nothing in common with them!"

September 25$^{th}$ arrived and true to my resolution, I left the house to spend the day with a girlfriend. I thought to myself, "That will serve them right, they will come and I won't be home!" By the time I came home in the evening, my home was full of people who were singing and dancing Greek folk dances. My mother, who loved to dance, was right there in the middle of the living room floor leading a dance. They saw

# BRIDGING THE AEGEAN

me arrive, turned to me and said, "We've been enjoying your Name Day, Frosula, *"Hronia Pola!"* (a toast meaning 'to many years') and went back to their eating and dancing. I felt stunned and deflated; I thought, "They didn't even miss me!" So much for my teenage rebellion about Name Days.

Frequently, we would be spending my Name Day in Antigoni (Greek name for the Turkish Island of Burgaz, off the coast of Istanbul.) The ritual of the day would begin with my maternal grandmother, Eleni, arriving on the 10:00 a.m. ferryboat from Istanbul carrying a cherry tart, my favorite childhood dessert. Nobody has ever made or will make cherry tarts as great as my grandmother's. She would only use cherries that she herself had marinated for months with a touch of cherry liqueur—also homemade.

I would go to meet the ferryboat way ahead of time, and would wait impatiently on the dock for looking for the familiar slight figure that was my grandmother, carrying her usual big pan of cherry tart. We would walk to the house, me admiring and smelling the tart and my grandmother beaming.

We went through this ritual for many years till one time my grandmother did not come. She had had a stroke the previous spring that left her speechless and without the ability to travel on the ferryboat or to make any more cherry tarts.

## Froso Hacipara Sendukas

Now some forty years later, I live in Houston, Texas and my Name Day is almost like any other day of the year. I may get an occasional phone call from a close friend who remembers the day's significance, but that's all. Mostly I get up and go to the office and listen to people's problems as I usually do and pretend that it's OK that not many people know or care about the day's special meaning for me. Even my grown children, who never forget to acknowledge my birthday or other holidays, do not pay any attention to September 25$^{th}$.

In earlier years I would occasionally bake a cherry tart on my Name Day, and even though it never tasted quite like my grandmother's, it would satisfy some of my nostalgia. What it could not do, however, was to quell the longing for what's no longer here: the blanket of love that my mother and grandmother would always stretch out for me, especially on my Name Day.

# BRIDGING THE AEGEAN

## MY MOTHER'S FAITH

My mother was a truly religious woman. She was religious in the best sense of the word; steadfast in her faith in good times and bad, but never fanatical. She always told me that all places where God is worshipped needed to be revered and treated with the utmost respect regardless of whether they were Greek Orthodox, Catholic, Jewish, Muslim, etc.

Once when I was about 13 or 14 years old, I went inside a Mosque on a bet from a friend who said that I didn't have the guts to do it. Eager to prove otherwise, I went in—not even noting that my head was uncovered and that I was wearing slacks (a big "no-no" for women entering a mosque). This happened on a small resort island off the coast of Istanbul called Burgaz, where my family and I spent most of our summers. I thought, "Who is to know?" No one stopped me as I walked around the mosque, which was empty at that time of the day. And then, hearing a faint noise in the back, I ran out, triumphantly telling my girlfriend who was waiting for me outside, that I had won the bet. She grudgingly agreed.

I thought that was the end of my little escapade, but I was as wrong as could be. When I went home late that evening, I found my mother furious at me, telling me that I was grounded for the week. This was not like my mother at all. She was a rather permissive parent who hardly ever scolded me, let alone punished me. I said, "What did I do? Why are you punishing me?" That's when I found out that the *muezzin* (a man who calls Muslims to prayer) in the mosque had seen me enter the place, giggling and laughing earlier that afternoon—when I thought the place was empty. "Did you forget that Mustafa Bey lives on our street?" she said, "He recognized you and came to tell me what you did. And you had the gall to be disrespectful and wear slacks on top of everything! How could you, Frosula? Haven't I always taught you to respect and honor all places of worship? I want you to promise me that you'll never do anything like that again!"

I was speechless with surprise and embarrassment. I had no idea that somebody had witnessed my juvenile prank and recognized who I was. As a result, from then on I was much more careful with my conduct in places of worship.

My education about respecting and honoring religious places continued. One of my mother's favorite activities was to visit out-of-the-way Greek Orthodox churches all over Istanbul. There were hundreds of small churches all over the city. Most were relics of the past, some dating back hundreds of years, from the time when Istanbul was called Constantinople and part of the Roman Empire ruled by Emperor Constantine. My mother would make sure to visit them on the feast day of the patron saint in whose honor the church or chapel was erected. If the feast day happened to be during a school holiday, she would take me along—or drag me along would be more like it. I knew better than to argue with my mother over going, she would look so distressed and hurt, I would feel immediately guilty and agree to go with her.

In fact, my earliest memory is of being lost on top of a hill outside a church in a remote area of Istanbul. I don't remember the name of the church. It seems my mother and grandmother were attending a *panagiri* (pilgrimage/feast day) in this church that was quite famous and attracted hundreds of Greeks from all over Istanbul and even some nearby cities and towns. I was 3 or 4 years old and my mother (she told me in later years) thought that my grandmother was watching me, so she went inside the church to help collect money (these little churches depended on their annual feast day for revenue, since their usual membership was very small.)

As my mother went inside, my grandmother saw some of her friends and went to talk with them. As she stood there animated and happy to be with friends she hadn't seen in a while, I must have let go of her hand and drifted away. She never noticed. Next thing I remember is being on another part of the hill, away from the familiar crowd and crying because I found myself among strangers. Women (the attendance was 90% women) kept asking me my name. I kept telling them my first name, but in fear of being lost and away from my mother, I couldn't remember my last name. Finally, some kind woman took me by the hand and led me inside the church where the service was still going on. She whispered to the priest and he interrupted the service (something almost unheard of) to announce that there was a lost child, and asked the congregation if they knew who I was. My mother, appalled by my pathetic appearance, rushed forward and picked me up in her arms. I cried even harder, probably with relief. My mother, holding me tight, started looking for my grandmother. She found her and started yelling at her that she was not to be trusted to look after me. My grandmother yelled back and I started crying again. Both Mother and Grandmother stopped fighting long enough to try to comfort me and told me I could have any candy or sweet I wanted. (there were dozens of vendors around who had set up outdoor shops just for the day.) After I enjoyed my favorite candy at the time—cotton candy—my mother sat with me and assured me that she would never let me get lost again. She seemed so distressed over what had happened that I told her that I believed her, that I was OK and not to yell at my grandmother any more.

Another church visit that stands out in my memory came some years later when I was in middle school and was on a school holiday. This was a much quieter occasion. Mother and I took a taxi to one of the old quarters of the city, quite far from our house. The taxi driver made so many detours in so many old cobble-covered streets that I started getting a little apprehensive about where he was taking us. I was amazed that my mother even knew how to direct the taxi to where we were going. He certainly didn't seem to have a clue. We eventually arrived in front of a building so old and dilapidated that I thought she had made a mistake! She told me not to worry, that she knew the place and had been there before.

## BRIDGING THE AEGEAN

There was no religious symbol on the building or on the door. No cross, no icon of a saint, nothing to indicate that this was a church of any kind. (In later years I thought I came to understand why. I believed that the Greek Orthodox Patriarchate of Istanbul did not want to draw attention to the multitude of these historical old churches so as not to draw unwelcome attention to them or have them demolished to give way to newer buildings. As long as they were obscure and halfway hidden, they were rather safe—at least that was my theory.)

Mother and I went inside the building. At first glance the place looked abandoned. It was so dark that I didn't know where to walk. Then a stranger appeared—seemingly from nowhere—and handed Mother a lit candle so that we could see our way. We started going down the narrow stairs, also dark, guided solely by our candle. We seemed to be all alone in this place. I started feeling kind of spooked, I never liked dark places anyway. Sensing my mood and trying to lighten it, my mother told me that we would soon reach our destination. I turned to her and said, "What is this place and how old is it? It looks like a catacomb or something! Does it date back to the Romans or what? And where is the chapel? I don't see anything but dark shadows!"

Before she could reply, I heard a stern voice saying in Greek, "Be quiet, young lady this is a sacred place and you need to be respectful!" And then I saw an old man dressed as a priest appear from the shadows. My mother patted my arm and said, "Be patient, Frosula. Keep walking and you'll see why we came." We came to the end of the staircase and I saw a narrow hallway. There was no electricity here either, but there was a bright light coming from the end of the hallway. I saw five or six older women, and the priest who had scolded me earlier, all squeezed into a very small space and all praying in front of a beautiful icon of a female saint. There were fresh white carnations all around the ornate gold frame of the icon, and a few tall white candles in antique candlesticks, providing an eerie but golden light to the area. Even to my childish eyes this was an awesome sight. I thought to myself, "That's probably how the early Christians, afraid of persecution, gathered to pray in secret!" I shivered with some ageless, nameless sensation. "That's Saint Irini, my mother whispered, "she was a martyr, you know."

After we left the chapel, she told me the story of Saint Irini (Irene). "Irini was the daughter of a Roman governor," she said. "As a young girl she dreamed that she had been chosen to teach about Christ. She did what the dream told her to do and started spreading the word about Christ. Soon her fame spread and a lot of people came to hear her teach about the new Christian religion. The Roman authorities also heard about her teaching and arrested her and tortured her extensively in efforts to make her give up her faith. She was beheaded on May 5. That's why we celebrate Saint Irini's Day on that day", added Mother, "and why our church reveres her memory as a martyr and saint."

Mother, needless to say, was a great believer in church going. She had the absolute conviction that her week would not go right if she did not attend services on Sunday or at least "light a candle" if she was late for services. My mother would never force me to attend services with her, but I knew how important my attendance was to her, I am kind of embarrassed to admit that as a kid at times I used her devotion to my advantage. I knew from experience that if I attended services with her, I was much more likely to get what I wanted, whether it was a special dress or a special occasion to go to. The truth was that I didn't really need to resort to this—as long as Mother had the money (and sometimes even when she didn't!) she would rarely turn down my requests. She would sacrifice and deny herself just to please me, her only child.

In later years when I was an adult myself, she would try to make me understand how she felt about her faith and about church going. "The best way I can describe the experience," she would say, "is to tell you that I look forward to church services with great joy—more so, let's say, than if I was going to a movie or play or any other entertainment. Do you understand, Frosula?"

Mother died on her way to a church service. She was 67 years old. Those who knew her well said to me that they couldn't imagine or wish for a better kind of death for her. Three of her girlfriends had gone to her house to pick her up for a special feast day service. It must have been some saint's special day, I suppose. She greeted them, ready to leave, and said, "I didn't feel well all night. I knocked on some neighbor doors in the apartment, but nobody heard me or answered the door. I don't know what's happening to me…" and then leaned forward and collapsed in one of her friend's arms, and that was that.

I was a long way from Istanbul when this happened—in Houston, Texas to be exact—and when I heard of her death, I was devastated. There was shock, sadness and some guilt that I was not physically close to her at the time to help her out. Maybe if she had been with me in Houston, I thought, I would have rushed her to a hospital and maybe she could have survived the fatal heart attack that she had. It pained me to think that she knocked on neighbors' apartment doors the night before she died, for help, and the doors stayed closed. My mother's friends told me of the circumstances of her death during her memorial service that I attended in Istanbul. They saw me crying and said to me trying to comfort me, "She died as quickly and as peacefully as a bird! (*San ena pulaki*) Be happy for that."

We also had a small memorial service for her in the Annunciation Greek Cathedral in Houston. Two of my children, Perry and Chris (her grandchildren) were there with me along with Vanessa, Perry's wife, the only granddaughter-in-law that my mother had ever met. It was a Saturday morning and the church was totally empty when we entered. There are no Greek services on Saturday unless it's a special church holiday.

In the vestibule of Greek churches there is a special place where church members light candles before they enter the church. There were no lit candles as our group entered. The church was totally dark until the priest turned on the lights. The service was short but meaningful, at least to me. As we left the church at the conclusion of the service I noticed to my great surprise that there were five candles lit in a circle. That was the way my mother always lit candles since my children were born—one for each child, one for me, and one for her.

I was so shocked to see the candles that I thought my grief was making me hallucinate. I nudged Chris, my youngest son, who was walking next to me. "Do you see what I see, Chris", I said? "Yes, Mom, there are five candles here, just the way Grandma used to light them. I wonder where they came from"? I shivered and whispered that I didn't know, but that it really didn't matter. Mother had often stated to me that her love for me was so great that no matter what happened to her she would always be with me, and she was keeping her word even after her death. I truly believed that. Through the candles she was sending me an important message; that she was here with us in spirit and not to despair about her death. I smiled and walked outside into the sunlight.

Froso Hacipara Sendukas

# BRIDGING THE AEGEAN

## THE DAY I MET THE NEXT-TO-LAST KING OF GREECE

It was April, 1952, the week of Greek Orthodox Easter. I was on vacation in Athens, Greece with my father, Dimitri, stepmother, Meri, and my half-sister, Tula, who was six years old at the time. I was all of eighteen years of age and already had a couple of suitors who had gone to my father (as was the Greek custom) to ask for my hand in marriage. Since I hardly knew the fellows, the prospect of marriage to either one of them did not exactly thrill me. My father, though surprised and somewhat flattered by the proposals (both men were prominent members of the Greek community), turned them quickly down saying that I was too young to get married, and anyway I was going to college in the fall! My suitors, it seems, were both startled by this announcement. Besides the blow to their respective egos, they were just amazed that I was planning to go to college. It was definitely not common for Greek girls in Istanbul, Turkey in the 1950s to go for higher education. A good marriage was what families hoped for and often still arranged. My father later told me, with pride in his voice, that his daughter was smart as well as pretty, and so this tradition did not apply in my case. As for me, I couldn't have cared less for marriage proposals at the time. College and maybe even a career in the future beckoned. I was even determined to travel to faraway places. If Prince Charming happened to come along later—great!

My mother had told me on numerous occasions that she had taken me to Athens and the island of Rhodes when I was three years old. We had visited my father who was there fulfilling his military duty as a Greek citizen at the time. But all I remembered from that visit was lots of white buildings, a blue sky, and waves in the ocean.

On Easter morning, (*Pascha*), the weather was beautiful, in the 70s with soft breezes blowing. There were flowers everywhere and lots of loud joyful music. Two days earlier the scene was totally different. There was definitely no joyful music in the streets of Athens. It was Good Friday (*Meyali Paraskevi*) according to the Greek Orthodox calendar and either because of religious/cultural traditions or government decree, there was no popular music to be heard anywhere, Greek or Western, on local radio stations. All you would hear in public places—coffee shops, restaurants, etc.—was either funereal or heavy classical compositions by Beethoven or Wagner that were deemed solemn enough for the day. Living as I was at the time in Istanbul, Turkey, a Muslim city in a Muslim country—where Greek Easter or other Christian holidays were not even publicly acknowledged—Athens, that Easter week of 1952 was an astonishing experience! I was seeing the whole population participating in religious festivities instead of what I was used to—an ethnic community having a semi-secret, private celebration. This was very big and very public, and the sights and sounds overwhelmed me.

On Good Friday, there was a solemn religious procession in the early evening through the main streets of Athens, led by black robed Greek priests holding lit candles and accompanying the sepulcher, heavily decorated with flowers (mostly white carnations) and being lifted in the air by black robed acolytes and altar boys. This ceremony was meant to recreate and commemorate the burial of Jesus. At eighteen, I was not particularly religious—though I did attend church services, my mother made sure of that. Yet, now, many years later, I still recall how thrilling it was to be part of the crowd on that day, to see all traffic stop for the procession, and to make the sign of the cross in the street—openly—with thousands of Athenians around me doing the same. Conversation stopped while the procession went by and all I heard for a while was the centuries-old Byzantine chanting and the traditional Holy Friday Lamentations, *Ta engomia*, I had sung in church every Good Friday since I was a little girl. The scene brought tears to my eyes and I felt at that moment that this was where I belonged, here in the streets of Athens.

On Easter Sunday the atmosphere in the streets was totally different. Instead of funereal music and Byzantine chanting, there were sounds of loud, joyful, popular music—both Greek and foreign tunes—drifting into the street from passing cars, coffee shops, portable radios, etc. There were lots of people walking and milling around, dressed in their Easter finery, joyfully shouting to family members and friends, "Kalo Pascha!" (Happy Easter)

My father told us over breakfast that he had heard from "a very reliable source" that the King of Greece, King Paul I, was going to make an appearance late in the morning in a certain park in Athens, in honor of the Easter holiday. Father wanted our family group to dress quickly and go with him to the park and see the King. Since my father loved to meet celebrities and photograph them; and had often said that he had scoops from reliable sources that turned out to be not so reliable after all. I didn't really believe that we were going to see the King of Greece that morning, but I went along with the plan, not wanting to hurt my father's feelings. I even pretended to be excited by the prospect of meeting royalty for the first time in my life!

I could see from the street as we approached the park that it was full of Athenians picnicking and enjoying the lovely weather and special occasion. I could also smell the traditional mouthwatering smells of Greek Easter, especially lamb, *arni*, as it was cooked either whole on a spit or being grilled on skewers as *suvlaki*.

There were two royal soldiers standing guard at the gate of the park, dressed in *fustanella* (the Greek formal dress for honor guards) checking those who were to enter the park to make sure that they had an invitation to come and meet the King. My heart sank when I saw them, fully anticipating my father's disappointment, since we had no invitations in our hands. My father seemed unperturbed. Holding his beloved Rolex camera in front of his chest, he told the royal guard that he was a famous photographer from *Constantinoupoli* (the Greek name for Istanbul), and that he was the official photographer of the Greek Orthodox Patriarch (the Greek equivalent of the Pope). I winced as I heard Father brag about his importance. He was definitely exaggerating his professional position. Yes, he was a well-known photographer in Istanbul; and yes, he had photographed the Patriarch on occasion, but

## BRIDGING THE AEGEAN

he certainly did not have an official title as the "photographer of the Patriarch". I was embarrassed—as usual—by my father's inflation of facts, but I quickly forgot my embarrassment when I realized to my great surprise that the royal guards bought my father's story and opened the gate to allow us into the park.

Next thing I knew I was close to a circle in the middle section of the park and this tall imposing gentleman, resplendent in a military uniform with gold epaulets and lots of medals was in the middle of the circle. Surrounding him were more royal soldier guards and a smiling Frederick March (a noted Hollywood actor of the time). I remember thinking, "Oh, my God. This must be the King of Greece!" I noticed that one of his attendants was holding a basket of beautifully decorated red and gold Easter eggs, and he would hand them to the King one by one so he could clank eggs with the invited guests according to the traditional Greek ritual. I heard him say, "*Hristos anesti,*" (Christ has risen.), and then each person would respond with, "*Alithos anesti,*" (He has truly risen.). I noticed that Frederick March kept smiling and not saying anything—obviously not understanding either the Greek language or ritual.

My father came to my side and said with a triumphant tone, "Didn't I tell you that the King of Greece was going to be in the park today and that we were going to meet him? Don't just stand there, Frosula, go closer to the King so you can clank Easter eggs with him." I must have looked at my Father with shock in my face and I remember mumbling something to the effect of, "Baba, I really don't want to get any closer to the King. This is fine, I can see him perfectly well from here." Just as I was finishing my sentence, I felt myself being propelled (or pushed, more likely) forward. I didn't know if it was my father or the crowd pushing me, but next thing I knew, I was face to face with King Paul I and he smilingly handed me a red Easter egg decorated with gold trim. I was shy and in too much shock to hear what he said to me, but I remember whispering, "Kalo Pascha, your highness," and that's when I heard my father's camera click as he took the picture he coveted—his daughter clanking eggs with the King of Greece!

Paul I died in 1964 and his successor, Constantine II, was deported in 1973. By a national referendum in 1974, the overwhelming majority of the Greek population voted to abolish the monarchy and become a presidential parliamentary republic. Forty-seven years after that fateful Easter morning of 1952, I still have the picture of a smiling teenage girl in a new green Easter suit clanking eggs with the next-to-last King of Greece.

# BRIDGING THE AEGEAN

## FIRST DATE, FIRST LOVE

His name was Stefan, and he was gorgeous. He had soulful brown eyes, and longish curly blond hair that kept falling into his eyes. I had heard that he painted and wrote stories. I admired his talents and thought he was an "artist"! Reportedly, he also had a temper that matched his talents—but I didn't care about that.

To my 16-year-old eyes, he was the man of my dreams. I was not the only one to think that, all the girls I knew fancied Stefan and kept trying to get his attention. I decided that in order to beat the formidable competition for his favors, I had to find a way to stand out from the giggling, fawning crowd of young women. Being a big fan of American magazines at the time, I had read in *Seventeen* magazine (my bible for all teenage manners) that one way to get a popular boy's attention was to purposely ignore him and that would pique his interest. I liked the idea—it seemed so new and clever.

From then on, every time I would see Stefan in the street or at a party or gathering, I would pointedly ignore him. Not only would I *not* greet him, but I would even turn my back on him. Looking back, my behavior seems manipulative and even silly, but he was only seventeen years old himself, and my technique worked. After a while, he started noticing me and even seeking me out.

One day, to my delight, he came to my side as I was walking with friends and asked me if I liked dancing. My heart started beating faster and I felt a wave of excitement envelop me, but I tried hard not to show my feelings. Still following my winning technique, I casually said something to the effect that I liked dancing but only if my dancing partner was skilled. I looked at him with what I hoped was a seductive, teasing look and said, "Are you a good dancer, by any chance?" He smiled and said, "Why don't you meet me on Sunday at the ballroom of the Yeşilköy Hotel and find out for yourself. There's a tea dance there every Sunday at 4:00 p.m."

I thought my heart would beat out of my chest, it was beating so hard and fast that I thought that he would surely hear it. I tried to act calm and cool and cast a nonchalant glance downward. "Why not?" I mumbled, "Dancing is good exercise, I'll meet you there."

I don't remember walking home. I was in some kind of stupor. During all the excitement of the exchange with Stefan, I forgot one important fact. At age sixteen, I was not allowed to date. On this issue, my parents' rules and ideas were not that different from those of my friends. Sixteen-year-old Greek girls (or Turkish girls, for that matter) just did not date at that time. If they did, they would do it secretly and keep it from their parents. In fact, my mother was more liberal than most parents. I was occasionally allowed to go to movies and parties with a group of friends, but only if Mother knew the friends and their families.

I tried desperately to figure out a clever strategy on how to present this prospective date to my mother. There was one further complication.

# BRIDGING THE AEGEAN

The ballroom that Stefan had invited me to for the afternoon dance was at a resort hotel one and a half hours from Istanbul by train.

Finally, after a lot of thinking, I decided to tell Mother the truth. Being an only child and the apple of my mother's eye, I was used to mostly getting what I wanted. Granted, I was careful not to abuse the privilege, I had always been a good student and was careful about coming home at reasonable hours. My mother would often tell me that her friends were envious of her, telling her what a wonderful daughter she had, and pretty as well.

So, I approached Mother with mixed feelings of trepidation and confidence, thinking that even though teenage dates were against the Greek community's norms, that she would not refuse me. She had been young once—surely she would understand how important Stefan's invitation was to me.

To my dismay, after she heard me out, she told me a very firm "No"! When I protested, she explained that she not only did not want my reputation in the community to suffer but more importantly, she would not agree to the plan because of the distance involved and the time of day. "It's not safe for a young woman your age to go off on a train by yourself and come back late in the evening. So, you're not going, and that's final!"

I walked off, went to my room, and cried my eyes out. I didn't sleep much that night. By morning, I had made up my mind. My mother's and the Greek community's archaic ideas were not going to stop me from going dancing with the man of my dreams! After all, the American magazines that I loved were telling me that in the US, girls were dating at even younger ages.

When Sunday finally arrived, I felt calm in my determination. For the first time that I could remember, I lied to my mother and told her that I was going to visit a girlfriend for the day, but that I would be home by dinner time. I went straight to the train station. Since I didn't know the schedule, I had to wait for an hour for a train to arrive that would take me to the resort town, <u>Yeşilköy</u>. I was even too excited to read, I just sat in a compartment lost in my thoughts. The one-and-a-half hours on the train seemed endless.

I finally arrived at my destination. I saw the long curly blond hair from a distance, and my heart did a little jitterbug dance. Stefan said that he was glad I had come, that he wasn't sure I would. I don't remember what I replied. I just remember that I had a fixed, silly smile on my face the whole time (I saw it reflected on every mirrored surface that I passed).

We went to the ballroom of the hotel where the tea dance was being held. I saw the hours of the dance posted, 4:00 to 9:00 p.m. I had a fleeting thought that I might be late for dinner at home, since we usually ate around 7:30 p.m., but I pushed the thought aside. I was too caught up in the present, and did not want to think about negative consequences.

I don't remember what I wore that day but I do remember what I ate. I had a "peach melba", one of my favorite childhood desserts. I read somewhere that it was named for a famous Australian opera star named "Melba". It looks elegant, but it's easy to make. You lightly cook fresh peaches compote-style, cut them in half and place a scoop of vanilla ice cream in the hollow part of each half. You serve the peaches by drizzling raspberry syrup over them and covering them with whipped cream. Fresh raspberries on top are optional.

Stefan and I danced every single dance. True to his boast, he was an excellent dancer. The band was a local band and not very good, but who cared? I still remember the song, "Again," that was a hit at the time; the band played it numerous times. It was a slow number and Stefan's arms felt heavenly. I thought that the song was the most romantic thing I had ever heard!

Soon, or so it felt, the dance was over. To my shock I realized that it was now 9:00 p.m. and I still had the train ride time before I could go home. I knew then for sure that I was in trouble and that there was no way I could talk my way out of this.

## Froso Hacipara Sendukas

We went outside and started walking toward the train station. Even though it was late September, it was a balmy evening, with a gentle breeze from the Sea of Marmara. I was still floating, buoyant from the wonderful afternoon. He told me that he had a great time and that I was a gifted dancer, and then he leaned over and kissed me. I thought I had died and gone to Heaven.

The train arrived at 10:00 p.m., the last train of the evening. I got on it, and since I was still walking on air, I did not even notice at first that there were very few people on the train. Being late September, the resort season was over. I sat down in a compartment where there was an elderly couple and a middle-aged man sitting by himself. After a few stops, the couple left the train and I was left alone with the man, who was sitting across the aisle from me. I was busy reading and trying to concentrate on my book. At one point, I lifted my head from my book and saw to my horror and shock, that the man was exposing himself to me. I was unable to move. I was afraid to stay and too afraid to leave thinking that he would follow me. Finally, after what seemed an eternity, a conductor come into our compartment. I gave him my ticket, made myself get up, and ran out into the passageway. I started looking frantically for a part of the train with some people in it. I found a group of young people and sat near them, still in shock over what happened. We came to the train station in Istanbul and I ran to the taxi stand, worried sick that the man in the train might be following me. Thankfully, he was nowhere around and I took a taxi home. I was shaking with fear, and also some anger, that my magical first date had been spoiled.

I looked at my watch as we were nearing my house and noticed that it was 12:00 midnight. By this time I was resigned to my fate and to whatever would happen at home. I was so relieved to be safe that I didn't even care about the consequences. I rang the doorbell and my stepfather opened the door. He took one look at me and then he slapped me. Since this man was ordinarily a very soft-spoken, gentle person who had never laid a hand on me before or even raised his voice at me, I was in shock again, for the second time that evening. "Your mother has been going out of her mind with worry," he said. "She thought you were in a ditch somewhere dead. She is running around in the streets, going to all your friends' homes asking if they have seen you." At that time household phones were rare in Turkey and we didn't have one. I ran crying to my room, physically and emotionally stinging from the slap and the events of the day. I was grounded for a month. I never told Mother what happened on the train. I was afraid if I told her about the incident with the man that she would never ever let me leave the house again.

This was my first and last date with Stefan. I never saw him again. I heard that he had reconciled with his ex-girlfriend and that they were engaged to be married.

## Froso Hacipara Sendukas

For a long time afterwards, every time I heard the song, "Again," being played anywhere, I would feel a tightening in my chest and my eyes would fill with unshed tears. Do I ever regret that eventful first date? Not on your life!

# BRIDGING THE AEGEAN

## THE ANEMIA SAGA

My mother was firmly convinced that I was fragile and anemic and that I needed special nutrition and care. The truth was, I was a healthy child, with just the basic, normal childhood diseases. No matter how many doctors tried to reassure my mother about my health, nobody could convince her that her only child was not anemic and iron-deprived.

One of her firm beliefs was that castor oil could be my salvation and the solution for my so-called "anemia". When her efforts to get me to drink it failed, (I had tried it once and found it so foul-tasting, that I resolved to never drink it again), she tried more devious techniques. I vividly remember the day she mixed castor oil with olive oil, and used that mixture as a salad dressing for my favorite Greek/Turkish salad of tomatoes and cucumbers, *çoban salatası*. I took one taste of the salad, and felt like throwing up. I guessed instantly what my mother had done.

It was several months before I could eat tomatoes and cucumbers again. It took me a longer time to forgive Mother for her devious tactics and for almost ruining my favorite salad for life.

Mother's belief that I was anemic came to a head when I started attending a private boarding school for girls called Notre Dame de Sion. The school was run by French-Catholic nuns, and had an excellent scholastic reputation, but was not particularly noted for having a gourmet cuisine.

## Froso Hacipara Sendukas

I was staying at the school during the week and going home on weekends. I was twelve years old, and it was the first time in my life that I was away from home for any length of time. I did not like it.

My parents were going through a painful divorce. It was painful for me too so our lives were in a considerable state of upheaval.

Looking back, my Mother's decision to place me in a boarding school must have had a lot to do with the divorce. Practical though that may have been, I was still dreadfully homesick and unhappy about the situation.

The school had some strict behavior rules that we had to follow "or else." One particular rule was that the students had to speak French at all times—even amongst ourselves and even if we were first-year students, with a limited knowledge of the language. If we were caught not speaking French, our penalty would be that we could not go home for the weekend, we had to stay at the school.

I disliked the "boarding" part of the school experience so much that I made sure to learn to speak in French as fast as I could so as not to incur the penalty.

We addressed the nuns as "soeur" (sister). They all wore long black robes and big white hats, their only adornment was a big crucifix, dangling from a long chain.

# BRIDGING THE AEGEAN

Our sleep routine started at 8 p.m. every weekday evening. The first step in the routine was "washing up". We had to undress to the waist and then wrap a big towel around the top of our chests and stand in front of a sink and wash our faces, necks and upper chests, all under the probing, vigilant eyes of the nuns. Hot showers were available only once a week, due to the scarcity and/or expense of hot water in the city.

If and when we passed the inspection of the supervising nuns, we had to put on our "regulation" night gowns or pajamas and get ready for bed. At exactly 9:00 p.m., the nuns would clap their hands, and that was our signal to turn off our bedside lamps and go to sleep. Since I was used to going to bed at home around 10:00 p.m. the sleeping deadline was quite early for me.

This wasn't the end of what I used to call the "sleeping ordeal." We, the boarding students, slept in dozens of rows of identical narrow iron beds, with only a small personal table between the beds. The nuns would take turns walking up and down the dormitory aisles, the sound of their heavy boots reverberated around the dormitory most of the night. Being a light sleeper, the sound of these boots—stepping on old, creaking wooden floors—would frequently wake me up during the night.

It's hard to decide what I hated the most about my nights at Notre Dame de Sion. Was it the public ritual of semi-nude cleansing in front of other students and nuns? Or maybe it was hearing the heavy footsteps that seemed to go on for hours? It could also have been the

## Froso Hacipara Sendukas

9:00 p.m. rigid bedtime and the identical, hard, iron beds we slept on with no personal decoration allowed.

I know one thing for sure—for me, the only child of a loving family, all the above regimentation was very hard to take. Oh, how I missed my room at home, with all my favorite belongings and my precious books!

The first year at the boarding-school was especially difficult. I remember crying at night for months, while trying to be quiet about it so the nuns wouldn't hear me.

To be fair, the crying wasn't just about being terribly homesick. The family that I was missing was not the same family that I left behind when I started boarding. A divorce had taken place, changing everything. There were two families now in my life, with different lifestyles and new characters, some more pleasant than others. Familiarity had given way to lots of adjustments and losses.

This was 1945, when divorces were quite rare in the Greek community of Istanbul, so there was also public gossip and innuendos to tolerate and try to ignore.

I was in grief, so the crying at night probably had to do with that as well as the homesickness.

# BRIDGING THE AEGEAN

On treasured weekends at home (i.e. Mother's apartment), I often complained to my mother about the school's sleeping arrangements, but she was not very sympathetic. She would say, "None of this can hurt you, with you being an only child, I have probably spoiled you through the years. The time at Notre Dame de Sion can be a good learning experience. And aren't you glad that you are learning French? And so quickly!"

My mother, who obviously had different priorities than I, would quiz me frequently about the school diet. I was a picky eater at the time and Mother was worried that I would dislike the food at the school and starve to death! At home, if I didn't like the food she was serving, she would always make me something that I did like, like lamb chop.

The frugal nuns gave us lots of grains, legumes and vegetables, but only a small amount of meat. In terms of nutrition and health, the school was definitely ahead of its time, though I suspect that the primary reason for the relative absence of meat on the menu was financial rather than health-oriented.

My mother, who did not seem to care about the school's sleeping arrangements, definitely did care about the menu and it was obvious to me that she did not approve of the nuns' culinary choices.

Given her reaction, I thought that she would call the school and complain, but I never dreamed that she would go to the lengths that she did.

One Monday, as we students lined up to enter the dining room for lunch, I saw to my great surprise and dismay, a familiar but unexpected figure standing in a corner, holding a covered plate of food—my mother! She saw me and approached with glee written all over her face. "Here's some lamb chops I cooked for you, Frosula," she said, "I have a doctor's prescription for them. The Mother Superior at your school gave me special permission to bring them to you—you need the iron, so eat!"

The taste of the lamb chops (one of my all-time favorite dishes) was greatly diminished by the laughter and merciless teasing of my classmates. For weeks and even months after my mother's special performance in Notre Dame de Sion's dining room, I was called "The Lamb Chop Girl." I dreaded the sight of girls approaching me to say, "Did you have your iron today, dear?" or "Are you going to call your mother to complain about the food, today?"

It took a lot of reasoning and even pleading with Mother to stop her weekly visits to the school dining room. At first, she told me to ignore my classmates' teasing. She would say, "They probably wish they could have lamb chops from time to time also."

# BRIDGING THE AEGEAN

I finally succeeded in getting my point across and got her to understand that I could survive without a lot of meat, but not with her "special" treatment; and to stop bringing me lamb chops at school. Years later, when I was living in the United States, married and expecting my first child, my obstetrician told me that I was mildly anemic and needed some iron pills. When I told Mama about what the doctor said, she seemed overjoyed rather than concerned.

"Haven't I been telling you for years that you were anemic?" she said, "What did your pediatrician and other doctors know in Istanbul? Finally, you found a doctor in America who told you the truth." I'm sure she felt totally vindicated.

Froso Hacipara Sendukas

# BRIDGING THE AEGEAN

## THE VENDOUZES

When I was a child I dreaded getting sick, mainly because my mother hovered around me constantly, asking me all day long how I was doing. As an only child, I usually enjoyed being the recipient of all that love, but not when I was sick.

Like all children, I had a sensitivity radar about the adults around me. I would sense her considerable anxiety about my being ill and would feel guilty and annoyed at the same time.

There was an additional reason why I dreaded getting sick. This reason had to do with a family ritual that inevitably accompanied any and all illnesses in our house. Grandmother Eleni, who did not live with us, somehow would hear I was sick and promptly arrive at our home bringing the ritual with her. Since neither we nor my grandmother had a phone at the time, it was always a mystery to me how the news of my sickness would spread so quickly. I loved my "Yiayia" and usually enjoyed her visits, but not when I was sick. I dreaded her coming over then because of what I called her "tools of torture." Their actual Greek name was *vendouzes*, and I hated them. These were suction cups made of heavy glass that would be heated—and to my great distress—would get inverted on my bare back. I would moan and groan, to no avail, while 5 or 6 vendouzes would land on my upper body. To make matters worse, I would be cautioned by both mother and grandmother not to move while this ordeal was going on, so the cups could stay anchored on my back and not fall off and break. After a few minutes of this, I would beg my mother—who was standing nearby with an anxious look on her face—to get the vendouzes off me. She would urge me to be patient, "Just a few more minutes, Frosula," she would say, "the whole thing will be over and you'll feel a lot better, I promise".

I hated the whole experience, especially the beginning and end of this so called "treatment," and kept asking Mother why I had to go through this torture time and time again. I was told that the theory was that vendouzes would suction out the germs and fever of whatever ailed me. As proof to the above theory, my mother would point out that I always looked and felt better after grandmother Eleni's ritual/treatment.

"Of course, I feel better afterwards," I would retort, "it's called 'relief'! I'm so happy that the ordeal is over and that grandmother is gone, along with her instruments of torture, that I *do* feel better".

Mother would laugh and say, "You are smart, Frosula, but not smart enough to convince me that vendouzes don't work".

After some years of this—with me going through the whole roster of childhood illnesses, including the dreaded whooping cough—a miracle happened (at least to me). Penicillin came to Turkey! A scientist named Alexander Fleming had invented this wonderful drug a few years earlier, but it took a while for the drug to be refined and stabilized enough so it could be distributed globally.

# BRIDGING THE AEGEAN

Our family doctor convinced my mother to try the new miracle drug instead of relying on old-fashioned home/folk remedies like vendouzes. I breathed a big sigh of relief. I thought, "Thank you, Mr. Fleming, wherever you are!" I was 10 years old, and delighted to get rid of the vendouzes.

Moving forward to forty-five years or so, with grown children and grandchildren of my own, I went to spend a week at a wellness health spa in Mexico, called Rio Calliente. Located ninety minutes from Guadalajara—the second biggest city in Mexico—the spa seemed to be hundreds of miles away from the hectic pace of any city. At the time, there was no television at the place and phones were not allowed. The diet there was organic—vegetarian and surprisingly tasty. The only "entertainment" at Rio Calliente consisted of lectures on health, etc., by visiting speakers, and the occasional showing of a classic black and white movie.

I loved this simple and restful spa and had been to it numerous times in the past, with excellent results for my physical health and mental health. The natural hot spring waters, coming from the mountain where the spa is located (hence the name), were the best possible medicine for my arthritis, with no side effects.

This time around, I arrived at the spa with severe muscle spasms in my back. I had high hopes, though, that the place would work its magic one more time, and that the painful spasms would disappear.

## Froso Hacipara Sendukas

However, when a couple of days went by and I was still in a lot of pain, I started getting discouraged. I confided my distress to a staff member that I knew from previous visits. She asked me if had ever consulted the Mexican doctor who was on call at the spa. When I told her that I never had, she suggested that I make an appointment to go see him. She added that he had an excellent reputation and that he practiced holistic medicine.

Feeling desperate about my severe back pain and not wanting to take muscle relaxers or tranquilizers, I decided to take her advice and go see the local doctor.

After carefully examining me, Dr. Montero told me that he knew what would help my back pain. "This is an effective but non-medical, alternative treatment," he said, "and I only know its Spanish name." I asked him what it involved, and he opened a valise and lo and behold, he showed me some heavy glass cups that looked remarkably similar to my grandmother's vendouzes of many years ago. I started laughing, and I became aware that Dr. Montero was looking at me strangely.

I told him of my childhood experience, and he smiled and said that his own grandmother had believed in them also. "Holistic medicine all over the world is rediscovering the wisdom of old home/folk remedies," he said, "Do you want to give them another try?" I nodded my head.

# BRIDGING THE AEGEAN

Dr. Montero lit some matches and quickly inserted them —one by one—inside the glass cups. When I saw what he was doing, I stepped back, questioning in my head my earlier decision to repeat my dreaded childhood experience.

Seeing my reaction, he said, "Don't worry, Ms. Froso, the cups are not going to burn you or hurt you!" Dr. Montero kept his word. The cups did not burn me or hurt me. However, the procedure was still uncomfortable for me, though not as bad as when I was a child.

I have to admit that the Mexican version of "cupping" did reduce some of my back pain and muscle spasms. So overall, I was glad I had gone to see Dr. Montero.

That night I dreamed of Grandmother Eleni smiling at me while holding a handful of shiny vendouzes in her arms.

Froso Hacipara Sendukas

BRIDGING THE AEGEAN

## THE GIFT

I was ten years old when I was given a treasure of a gift. Actually, at the time of the gift, I did not think of it as a treasure but I certainly have since. This was not a material gift—no money ever exchanged hands—and at the time, it was not even identified as a gift. It was introduced casually as an invitation to visit my neighbor's library. That casual invitation transformed itself into a life-changing force that expanded my mind for years with never-ending vistas of discovery.

The library in question belonged to an elderly, childless Greek couple that had just moved into our apartment building, Mr. and Mrs. Kondroulis. When they first arrived, my mother went over to welcome them carrying her usual gift—flowers. She also dragged me along, much to my dismay, not suspecting that these strangers would play such an important part in my life.

They greeted us warmly, thanked Mother for the flowers, and then asked how I was doing in school. My mother quickly replied that I was an excellent student. Mr. Kondroulis then asked me if I liked to read. I told him that I loved to read. He smiled and said, "Come, then, let me show you our library room." We all walked to the back of their apartment and I stared wide-eyed. What a glorious room that was! The only furniture in the room were floor-to-ceiling bookcases crammed with millions of books (or so it seemed to my childish eyes) and one comfortable reading chair, period. The books mesmerized me, and I had a hard time pulling my eyes away.

Mr. Kondroulis turned to me and said, "Frosula, why don't you come over some afternoon and spend some time in our library? You can read whatever you want; the only condition that I have is that you do your reading in the library room. You cannot remove the books from here or take them home, ever."

I looked at my mother, asking with my eyes for permission and she said, "Why not? As long as you don't bother Mr. and Mrs. Kondroulis, go ahead and take advantage of their kind invitation." I was not too surprised by my mother's response. She came from a poor background, had only an 8th grade education, was largely self-taught, valued education highly, and had always encouraged me to read.

That's how it started that I had access to a treasure on an almost daily basis. Most afternoons I would come home from school, hug my mother, and then rush downstairs to the Kondroulis' apartment. We soon developed a ritual of sorts. I would go to the wonderful library room with all the tomes that I soon came to regard as precious friends and I would delight in choosing and reading books from the vast selection before me. I would sit there for hours. My hosts would never disturb me or even come into the library room during the time I was there. I was never asked what I was reading, the selection was totally up to me.

# BRIDGING THE AEGEAN

Around 5:00 p.m. I would hear a timid knock on the door and Mrs. Kondroulis would appear with a tray in her hand, asking me if I wanted to join her and her husband for cookies and lemonade. I would take refreshments with them and as soon as I could politely take my leave, I would rush back to the library room, close the door and resume my reading. Around 7:00 p.m. I would hear my mother's voice at the apartment door summoning me to dinner. Thankfully, Mother would never ask about my reading selections either. It would never occur to her to censor my reading material, she was just happy for me to be doing any reading at all.

It actually was a good thing for me that no adults at the time ever questioned my reading selections. It is important to mention here that there were no children's books in the Kondroulis library, all the books were adult fiction and non-fiction. They ranged from famous works of literature, Shakespeare, Dickens, Dante, all translated into Greek, of course; some semi-historical novels about the Byzantine and Ottoman Empires, the latter ones in Greek, Turkish and French. Years later when I was in college, reading my first Shakespearean love sonnets in English, I thought they looked vaguely familiar. Then I remembered that I had first read the Greek translations in my treasure room.

A lot of the books I was reading would, I'm sure, not be considered suitable reading material for a ten-year-old child by educators and/or many parents. However, I truly do not believe that the reading harmed me in any way. To the contrary, it not only made me a better student, especially in the subjects of literature and history, but it also gave me a gift for life—a passion for books!

By the time I was twelve years old, I had run through a considerable number of books. The only volume that I found daunting and did not read past the first few pages was Homer's Odyssey in ancient Greek. It was so hard to understand that I put it aside for a later time; the rest of the books were fair game. I especially delighted in the novels about the emperors of the Byzantine era and the sultans of the Ottoman Empire. I would skip the sexual scenes described in the more lurid of the genre. I guess I was too young to get any pleasure out of that; but I would spend hours reading about court intrigues, harem girls, etc. The hours I spent in the Kondroulis' library were the highlight of my life!

At twelve, I started attending Notre Dame de Sion, a private school in Istanbul run by French nuns. I was there for three years. After a few months at the school, I remember thinking, "Aha, now I can start reading the French books at my private library." The nuns were amazed at how quickly I learned to read and write the French language. Looking back I have no doubt that the idea of access to hundreds of French books was a prime motivator in learning the language so quickly.

That was also the year of my parents' divorce and my father's remarriage. To add insult to injury, I had to appear pleased about the birth—soon after—of a squalling baby girl, Tula, that I was told was my new half-sister! Since I had been an only child till then, and the apple of my father's eye, I naturally was not thrilled about the new competition for my father's affections.

My salvation and escape from dealing with all these disturbing changes in my life, once again, was the Kondroulis library. I would get totally wrapped up in all the fictional adventures that I was reading and forget, at least for a while, the emotional chaos in my family life.

I still remember some of the thousand and one tales about the emperors and the sultans. One unforgettable love story that I read was about Emperor Justinian and Theodora, a woman of humble origins. She was what we would call nowadays an "exotic dancer." In fact, she was the exotic dancer of her time. Her seductive dancing in scanty attire, and her erotic antics on and off the stage earned her a certain kind of fame throughout Byzantium. In the books I read, historians called her a harlot and/or a courtesan (I didn't know what those words meant at the time; after all I was only ten or eleven years old when I first read about this, but I quickly looked up the words.) Justinian, who, at the time was heir to the Byzantine throne, heard about Theodora's fame and went to see her dance—the rest, as they say, is history. He became so enamored of her that he married her, despite the strong objections of his court advisors who told him he might lose the throne due to public indignation. Nothing would deter Justinian. He even passed a law legalizing marriage with a prostitute, until then forbidden by Roman law.

## Froso Hacipara Sendukas

It was under Justinian's rule that the famous church of Haghia Sophia was erected. Other churches had been started at the same site, but his was the first to be completed. It has become one of most outstanding examples of Byzantine architecture in the world, as well as an everlasting symbol for Greeks everywhere of their identity and faith. I remember reading of his accomplishment, but what made a lasting impression on my young mind was his passion for Theodora and how he made her, against all odds, his empress. I had no aspirations at the time to ever become an exotic dancer and/or courtesan, but I have to admit to some daydreaming back then about having the kind of charms that would entice a man to go to such considerable lengths for me!

Another tale that I still remember some fifty years later is that of the Greek slave girl during the era of the Ottoman Empire who was chosen to become part of Sultan Abdul Aziz's harem. She became so distraught, that late at night, she tied two heavy stones to her feet and drowned herself in the dark waters of the Bosphorus. Was this tale true? I have no idea. I do know that the story led to further daydreaming about whether I would have had the courage—under similar circumstances—to kill myself rather than submit to a sultan's sexual advances.

There are no emperors or sultans in Turkey anymore, they are long since gone. However, these tales and hundreds of others that I read did make Turkey's past come alive for me in a way that no history class in my various schools ever did.

And then I was fourteen and the unthinkable happened. My mother announced that she was getting remarried and that we were moving from our apartment to one across town, in a newer subdivision of Istanbul. I remember asking her, "But how am I going to go to the library and read my books? It's too far to walk, we have no car, and there is no public transportation between the old apartment and our current one." "Don't worry, Frosula", she said, "soon you will transfer to the preparatory department of the American College for Girls. I'm sure that they will have a wonderful library there, it will make you forget all about the Kondroulis library." I wanted to cry out, "I bet the new school doesn't have any books on Sultan Abdul Aziz and his harems!" But I didn't say what I was thinking. I was afraid that my words would shock Mother and make her regret her lack of censorship about my reading material.

My mother later told me that Mr. and Mrs. Kondroulis cried when she told them we were moving. They told her that my going to their house and using their library gave them a great deal of pleasure; they saw me as the daughter they never had. That's when I understood why they had been so insistent that I read their books in their library and not take them home. When I was ten years old, I had thought that they didn't trust me to return their books and that's why they had the stipulation of my having to read the books in their library. At fourteen, I finally understood that the issue was not about a lack of trust at all. Rather, it was because they were lonely and wanted the presence of a book-loving child in their apartment, even though I only spent about half an hour a day in their presence, having cookies and lemonade.

I didn't know it back when I started going, but I had a gift to give them as well.

# BRIDGING THE AEGEAN

## A GODLY MAN

I had just turned fifteen on that January 1949 morning when Mother announced that we were going early to church on Sunday because it was an important historical occasion for the Greek community of Istanbul and for all other Greek communities all over the world. I was listening to her, vaguely interested; at fifteen, my girlfriends and I were much more preoccupied with catching the eye of a cute boy than in celebrating historical occasions.

"This is truly a special day", my mother added (ignoring my lack of enthusiasm for her news). "I do not want you to miss it. The new Ecumenical Patriarch Athenagoras (the Eastern Orthodox religion's equivalent of the Pope) is going to celebrate his first liturgy in a local church."

Of course, I knew who she was talking about. Our whole community was abuzz about the news. Not only was he the new elected Patriarch but he had arrived with a lot of charismatic baggage preceding him. We knew that he had been a popular Archbishop of North and South America for 17 years, Rumor was that he was even a personal friend of the President of the United States, Harry Truman. After all, had he not arrived in Istanbul after his election, in a presidential plane? The small local Greek newspapers were full of news pertaining to the fact that President Truman had provided the US Air Force DC 4 as a gesture of goodwill and respect to Patriarch Athenagoras and members of the Greek Orthodox Church in America and elsewhere. Truman had even assigned an Air Force liaison office from the White House to be the Patriarch's official escort on the post-election trip to Turkey.

How we swelled with pride as we heard and read all these reports! How important we felt for a moment in time to be Greek! In all the usual places that Greeks congregated: The Hellenic Center in Pera, churches, coffee shops, restaurants, etc., the favorite topic of conversation for many months that year was Patriarch Athenagoras and his powerful connections in the United States.

Even the Turkish press, who generally ignored news pertaining to their minority (Greek) population, and would speak with some condescension of the Patriarch in Istanbul, this time mentioned the fact that the new Patriarch had arrived from New York via Presidential plane! They were quick to add however that the plane, formerly used by Presidents Roosevelt and Truman, had been replaced as President Truman's principal aircraft a couple of years before and was no longer the official Air Force One.

What did we care about small details like that? We reveled in the circumstances of his arrival and hoped that some of this would rub off on all Greeks and strengthen our status as minority citizens in Turkey.

Sunday arrived and Mother and I went to meet the new Patriarch. The church service was held at a local church called "Panaghia" (the Virgin Mary). I am guessing that this particular church was chosen because of

# BRIDGING THE AEGEAN

its history (one of the oldest Greek churches in Istanbul) and its central location in Beyoğlu (Pera in Greek, a main street of Istanbul in an area where many Greeks resided at the time), and also because it had a large and beautiful courtyard that was reached by climbing some old marble stairs on a side street.

The place was so crowded that even though we were early, we had a hard time even reaching the vicinity of the church. People were lined up in the street around the church and we couldn't even come close to the stairs.

However, my mother had come to meet the new Patriarch and she was a determined woman, especially in matters of her religion and faith. She took one look at the long line of people and turned to me and said, "Frosula, I know I taught you to be nice and polite at all times but today I'm going to ask you to forget my teachings and shove your way as close to the church as you can. Just do it nicely, of course; don't hurt anybody!"

So we pushed and shoved (always nicely, of course) and we finally arrived by the doors of the church. As we arrived closer, I noted that my father (who by then was already divorced from Mother)—a photographer of some reputation and note in Istanbul, and owner of a local photography shop called Foto Sehir—was already positioned by the door with his beloved Rolex camera aimed high, ready to photograph the Patriarch as he emerged from the church. By this time, the service was almost over. There was no way we could actually get inside the church, so we stood in the courtyard and waited along with hundreds of other Greeks. Excitement was high and hope was palpable that morning! Somebody told Mother that a couple of elderly women had fainted in the crowd. I felt a little guilty then about all of the shoving I had done, but I got over the feeling as the doors of the Panaghia church swung open and the Patriarch came out to meet the crowd.

I'll never forget my first glimpse of him; he had such an imposing presence! He was quite tall for a Greek, over six feet. We could see him above the crowd. He had a long grayish-white beard that covered half his chest. In his white and gold silk robes holding a jeweled scepter with a huge cross around his neck, he looked every inch the Patriarch of a hundred million Orthodox faithful around the world. There was a roar from the crowd in the courtyard when they first caught sight of him and then as he started speaking, total silence fell over that previously noisy, boisterous Greek crowd.

He started speaking without a microphone, in a strong, melodious voice and even I, a somewhat self-centered teenager who had previously been looking around the crowd to locate friends, stopped looking and started listening. Fifty years later, I still remember some of what he said. He told us that he was happy to be with us and honored to be serving the world of Orthodoxy from this ancient seat called Constantinople in the past and Istanbul presently. He emphasized that it was important to remember its present name (that was an interesting comment to make given that Greeks continually called their city Constantinople). He also expressed hope that the Greek citizenry's relations with the Turkish government would be cordial and mutually respectful, and that he would do everything in his power to bring this about.

And he tried; boy did he try! In the past the Greek Orthodox Patriarch was hardly visible in the public eye, except for Church holidays—and even then, in order to see him we had to go to Phanari, (an old residential section of Istanbul where the Patriarch was located). Athenagoras refused to follow the traditional path. He would not be confined to that old quarter and to his official residence and offices, nor keep a low profile as was expected of him. In the months that followed his arrival, we could see pictures of him in both the Turkish and Greek press with a notation that he was appearing in some public event or other; even official events that had nothing to do with Greeks per se. We suspected that he often went without being invited by the mayor of Istanbul or other city officials, (since there had been no previous pattern and/or tradition of formally inviting representatives of Christian or other faiths to public events). Christian priests in Turkey's past had always tried to be as inconspicuous as possible, especially the Patriarchs! Maybe the ghosts of the past were still with them, especially that of Patriarch Gregorios.

At dawn on Easter Day, 1821, Patriarch Gregorios was officiating a liturgy in the cathedral when he was summoned by Turkish officials and taken before the Holy Synod in the Phanar with a charge of conspiracy against the Ottoman Empire. He was deposed as Patriarch, and a few hours later was hung from the gate of the Patriarchate with a note attached to his chest accusing him of being a traitor to the Ottoman Empire. Authorities gave his body to a group representing the local Jewish community with orders to throw it into the sea after dragging it through the streets of the city. George Young, in his book Constantinople says there is a Greek legend to the effect that the body was found the next morning mysteriously floating next to a Greek vessel. The actual historical explanation is less mysterious and more touching. The Jews secretly surrendered the body to representatives of the Greek community and Patriarch Gregorios was buried with honors as a martyr of the Greek Orthodox faith.

There had been other Patriarchs through the last hundred years that had either been expelled or stripped of any importance and prestige by past Turkish governments. However, our new Patriarch seemed oblivious to all the tumultuous history of his predecessors. Instead of being inconspicuous, he would appear in full regalia with his flowing robes and religious adornments. And even in the simple black clerical robes that he had to wear in public (unless he was officiating a service), he would still manage to look imposing and even regal at his full height of 6'4" and long luxurious beard. We, his fellow Greeks, admired his self confidence and bravado but held our collective breath and started worrying— about him, and maybe in retrospect, about ourselves. Did he not know where he was? This was Istanbul, Turkey, not New York.

Wasn't he aware of possible consequences? Along with pride, some Greek journalists started expressing in print the ambivalent feelings of the community that were whispered around town, and urged some caution. "Do not be so obvious," they said. "Your behavior may seem deviant and provocative." Other Greek journalists liked what he was doing but advised him not to trust the Turkish government and to tone down his comments about friendly relations between the Greek community and the authorities. Once again Greeks were being typically Greek and true to their heritage from Aristotelian times to the present, indulging in one of their favorite pastimes—hotly, passionately, debating issues. Or as some objective (obviously non-Greek) observers might say: "Arguing with each other in the press, at gatherings and in the streets of Istanbul."

Patriarch Athenagoras at first seemed oblivious to our concerns and internal politics of the community. As time went by, however, and as Turkish officials ignored his friendly forays and snubbed him in public, his public appearances became less and less frequent. After a while the resplendent flowing robes gave way to austere black and the large Patriarchal jeweled cross that he had always worn was not so visible any more, except when he was celebrating liturgy. The charismatic presence and confidence that he had first exuded upon his arrival in our city as the new Patriarch seemed to dim with time and exposure to Turkish politics.

## Froso Hacipara Sendukas

We noticed these changes and understood the reasons for them but I remember that even as a teenager, I had mixed feelings about the situation. "He is a very intelligent man," I thought and as such he adapted to the situation and probably listened to his advisors and journalists who were urging caution and less visibility. I, for one, missed the charisma and bravado of the early days and almost defiant participation in public events despite the indifference and even shunning by officials that he experienced. I guess, looking back, I wanted to believe that the hope of new beginning and positive changes for the Greek community in Istanbul would still materialize and be palpable in the air. "Too bad that the reality of the situation wore him down," I thought, and felt sad.

Then Easter arrived as usual that spring. Easter is the most important Greek holiday of the year, even more important than Christmas. One Turkish newspaper, Cumhuřiyet (The Republic) that happened to be the most serious newspaper in the city and seemed to us to be more fair toward minorities than other more sensational local newspapers, placed a small but prominent insert in the paper wishing the Greek Community a Happy Easter. We rejoiced and showed the newspaper to each other, thinking that maybe times were changing. Again hope filled our hearts and we wondered if the new Patriarch's presence in Istanbul (after all, he had been friends with the American President) was having a salutary effect on Turkish-Greek relations.

# BRIDGING THE AEGEAN

For as long as I could remember, my family's custom was to go to a nearby Greek church for midnight Easter services. The church was so close to our house, a few blocks away, that we walked there. When I was a little girl, Pascha (as Easter is called in Greek) was traditionally held outside, in the courtyards of churches and every parishioner would hold a tall candle that was lit exactly at midnight, to symbolize the resurrection of Jesus. Then we would sing the hymn "Christos Anesti" ("Christ has Risen") over and over again. I loved to sing that hymn! Then after the service ended (and sometimes earlier, since the Greek Orthodox Easter Service tends to go on till at least 2:30 a.m. and I would get very sleepy as a child) we would go home, on foot again, holding the lit Easter candles in our hands. It was considered a sign of good luck in the Greek community to be able to bring the candle home without allowing the flame to go out. When we reached our home, we would make a sign of the cross on the door with the strongest candle, the one whose flame had survived the journey. As a child I remember praying for good weather that night so my candle would make it home OK. Sometime between my early childhood years and adolescence, a new Turkish law was passed that forbade outdoor religious celebrations. Since we didn't know any other religion that had a traditional outdoor service, we suspected that the law was aimed at Greek Easter, but of course we couldn't prove it or do anything to protest and/or fight the law.

Since the law did not mention anything about lit candles in the street, we continued to walk home with the candles in our hands. It was quite a sight to see hundreds of individuals and families light the way to their neighborhoods and homes late into the night. The year of Patriarch Athenagoras' arrival, my mother, stepfather and I decided to attend Easter midnight services at the very old and historic Chapel of the Patriarchate in the Phanar section of Istanbul. Since we lived about 45 minutes by car from the Phanar, I remember not being thrilled by the idea. The Phanar, at one time, many years ago, had been the premier residential address of Greeks in the city. Even when Constantinople became Istanbul and was run by the sultans of the Ottoman Empire, it was still a source of pride for Greeks to call themselves "Phanarioti" (resident of Phanar). But that was a long time ago. Occasional fires had ravaged the area and most Greeks, once they could afford it, had moved through the years to newer, more central and better kept suburbs of Istanbul like Pera, or picturesque towns around the Bosphorus. The old quarters of the city like Phanar had grim stone buildings and streets that were hard to walk on because of numerous pot holes. To me, the area looked dark and unpleasant despite some wonderful views of the city that tourists would exclaim over. I shared my misgivings with my Mother who assured me that we would go by taxi (like most residents of Turkey, we didn't own a private car) with a chauffeur that she knew and trusted and that we would be perfectly safe. She emphasized that we were going for an important reason—to honor Patriarch Athenagoras as he celebrated his first Easter Service in our city.

When we arrived for services, we realized that a lot of other Greeks had the same idea that we had. The Church was packed. This was not my first time there—my Mother had brought me there on other occasions, but it had been a while since I had visited there. I was struck once again about the unique beauty of the historic Chapel. Neither new nor renovated, it did not look like any of the Churches that I regularly visited. However it had obviously been spruced up for the occasion, and the ancient icons glowed by candlelight. There were lots of Easter lilies by the altar, looking festive and beautiful. Since I was a very young child, I have always loved Greek Easter services. I don't believe there has been a year when I missed one. I especially love it when the Church goes totally dark a few minutes before midnight (except for a small light inside the altar that stays lit) and then the Priest says, "Lavete fos" (Let there be light) and then a lit candle passes from the Altar to all the pews and people start handing over their candles to be lit, and soon after the Church is lit with the flames of hundreds of candles. The spectacle always fills me with wonder and joy and such strong emotions that, as I've gotten older, tears always come to my eyes (nowadays, I remember my Mother and all the Easters of my childhood as I light my candle). Then the Easter hymn "Hristos Anesti" is sung numerous times and only then does the regular service begin. By this time, some leave the Church service and one can hear joyful greetings of "Hristos Anesti" and "Alithos Anesti" (Christ has risen) and the response—"He is truly risen").

Because of the ban against outdoor religious activities, the Easter liturgy that we attended was celebrated inside the Patriarchate Chapel. Unlike customary Greek behavior, I noticed that on that particular night very few people left shortly after midnight. I suspected that most, like our family, stayed throughout the long and late service so that at the end we would be handed "blessed" red eggs by the Patriarch himself. (At the end of most services the officiating Priest hands out "bread" that has been blessed called "andithero", but on Easter that changes to red eggs).

As we approached the altar around 2:00 AM, I looked at the Patriarch. The imposing presence was still there and so were the piercing but soft eyes, but did I imagine a new sadness in his eyes?

The next time I was to look at the Patriarch's eyes was some years later, in September of 1956 to be exact, a few days before I left Istanbul, Turkey to come to the U.S.A. on a student visa—ostensibly to continue my studies, but in reality I was coming to join my Fiancé who was already in the States. We were to get married and live in the U.S., at least for a few years before deciding whether to stay or not.

My Father, who had photographed the Patriarch on several occasions in the past, had pulled every string in his possession and arranged for a private meeting with Patriarch Athenagoras so he could give me his blessings for this eventful journey. I was a little nervous before the meeting but His Holiness was very gracious and quickly put me at ease with his demeanor. He still had the same regal presence, but I thought he looked a lot older since I had seen him a few years earlier, and there was no question that the sharp, piercing eyes now looked sad. After all, the anti-Greek riots that had devastated the local Greek community had just occurred a year ago (September of 1955) and had changed forever what it meant to be Greek in Turkey.

There were four of us in that room. Besides my Father and I and the Patriarch, there was also a Greek Priest (an assistant to the Patriarch I presumed), who remained silent throughout the meeting.

I do not remember details of that meeting, except that it was conducted in Greek and that during the meeting the Patriarch gave me a letter to give the Greek Priest of the New Orleans parish. He told me the letter was meant to introduce me as a member in good standing of the local Greek community. I took the letter, thanked him and briefly wondered about how surprised the Louisiana Priest would be getting a letter from the Patriarch. It would be like a U.S. Catholic Priest of any city in the U.S.A. getting a personal letter from the pope himself about a new member of the parish.

I do not remember anything else that happened during the meeting, but I vividly remember how the meeting ended. My Father and the assistant Priest left the room first. I went over to Patriarch Athenagoras to kiss his hand (a traditional Greek gesture of respect towards Priests) and thank him for his blessings and for the meeting. Suddenly, unexpectedly he leaned his head towards me and whispered to me in English, "I envy you, young lady, you are going to the land of freedom." and then he walked away, leaving me stunned.

## Froso Hacipara Sendukas

Athenagoras died in July 1972 in Istanbul. He was 85 years old. He had come to Turkey from the USA as elected Patriarch in 1948 with many goals and many hopes riding with him on that fateful Air Force One flight. He had been accorded more respect in New York as Eastern Orthodox Archbishop of North and South America than as a Patriarch in a Moslem country surrounded by a rather hostile government and citizenry. He never complained—at least not in public. The only time that I remember that he was outraged was in the aftermath of the 1955 anti-Greek riots in Istanbul. Even then his outrage was muted (I'm guessing so as not to bring any more misfortune to the Greek population). I have a picture of him touring the vandalized Churches and looking at the relics of Orthodox Saints thrown carelessly and wantonly on the ground. In the picture his head is bent low, I imagine so as to hide the tears in his eyes. His greatest achievement during his tenure as Patriarch was meeting with Pope Paul the VI in Jerusalem and the Vatican in an attempt to reconcile some of the differences between the Catholic and the Eastern Orthodox religions that had lasted for centuries. The historic meeting between the two religious leaders resulted in the mutual lifting of ex-communication.

The other goal—the one he had stated when he was first elected to his office, namely to improve relations between the Turkish government and the Greek community, proved to be a lot more elusive. This was probably due to the ongoing, bitter dispute between Turkey & Greece over the island of Cyprus, and the ancient feuding between the two countries that eventually culminated in the anti-Greek riots and the Greek exodus from Turkey.

Patriarch Athenagoras, despite what must have been some devastating setbacks to his goals during his tenure of office, never once lost his dignity in public or let people forget that he was the Ecumenical, religious leader of millions of Eastern Orthodox faithful all over the world. He did not indulge in recriminations or ugly name calling, even when provoked.

He gave me and fellow Greeks a wonderful example of what it truly means to be a man of peace, a man of God.

Froso Hacipara Sendukas

*My grandmother, Eleni Moshos*

*Me, fat cheeks and all, with my beautiful mother*

## Froso Hacipara Sendukas

*In my school uniform*

*Mother and me in Instanbul*

# BRIDGING THE AEGEAN

*My father, Dimitri*

*Me with childhood friends, around age 15, in Yeşilköy*

# Froso Hacipara Sendukas

*My half-sister, Tula, in Athens 1*

*College graduation in Instanbul with Mother and stepfather*

# BRIDGING THE AEGEAN

*First year in U.S., 1956*

*Clacking eggs with the next-to-last King of Greece, King Paul I*

# Froso Hacipara Sendukas

*My parents' wedding, (Anastasia & Dimitri), 1932*

# BRIDGING THE AEGEAN

## THE VULNERABILITY OF YOUTH

I feel so sad when I see and hear on TV or in the newspapers of the countless young women victimized by sexual harassment or molestation or worse by men having power or authority over their lives. First I get sad, and then I get angry. It happens all over the world all the time and I wonder "Is this ever going to change or stop?"

I'm sure that part of the sensitivity of my feelings on this subject has to do with my personal history. Despite the fact that I led a pretty sheltered life as the only child and daughter of middle class Greek parents, I still felt the sting of harassment as well as attempted molestations. I don't know that the incidents had anything to do with ethnicity, religion, or age, but it happens that all the aggressors were older Turkish men who at the time held some position of power or authority in my life.

The first incident occurred when I was fourteen years old. I had been going to an orthodontist to have my front teeth straightened. Since he was the only certified orthodontist in Istanbul at the time, he was also quite expensive. It had taken me quite a while to talk my Father into having the necessary treatment. He kept telling me that he couldn't afford the high fees and that I looked fine the way I was. I asked my Mother to intervene on my behalf and he finally agreed to take me.

I remember feeling jubilant the first time my Father and I went to the dentist's office. I did not even worry about any discomfort or pain that would inevitably come with braces. "The heck with the discomfort," I thought; I just wanted my teeth fixed. I was thrilled to see my Father agree to the financial terms and sign a contract.

At first my mother or father would come with me to the appointments, but after a while, I started walking by myself. I had been going to see Dr. Omar for a few months and was getting used to his cold personality and curt manner of interacting. The only person in the office who would chat with me at all was his dental assistant, a pleasant and friendly Turkish woman. There were no other employees.

One day I walked into Dr. Omar's office and noticed his Assistant was not there. I was disappointed not to see her and asked if she was sick. Dr. Omar replied in his usual curt manner that she was buying some office equipment. I didn't think anything of it and sat in the usual dental chair and opened my mouth ready for my braces to be adjusted. To my surprise and dismay, he didn't even glance in the direction of my mouth. He started stroking my lower stomach telling me that he had admired me for months and what a pretty young woman I was becoming. I was so shocked by the behavior and his words that I felt paralyzed in my chair. As he was looming over me, I felt trapped both physically and mentally. Both the stroking and the complimentary words felt rather pleasant at first in a hypnotic sort of way and I felt incapable of moving a muscle or saying anything.

# BRIDGING THE AEGEAN

The stroking got more intense and he started placing his hand underneath my sweater and that jarred me and made me realize what was happening to me. I shouted in Turkish, "*Yeter!*" *(Enough!*) and felt a stab of fear that nobody would hear me and come to my aid. A few seconds later, the door burst open and Dr. Omar's Assistant rushed in. He immediately withdrew his hand from my body, looked at her sternly, and said, "What are you doing here? I did not call for you at any time. Don't you know you have to knock before entering my office? Have you forgotten you are my employee?" I don't remember what her reply was. Taking advantage of her entrance, I jumped up from the dental chair, said, "I have to go home," and ran from the office. I was trembling when I got to the street on my way home. Nothing like this had ever happened to me. I was in shock.

I was in turmoil about the incident for weeks. I didn't know what to do. Telling my Mother or Father what happened was out of the question. I somehow knew that if I told them the truth, they would never allow me to visit Dr. Omar any more, and I also knew that my teeth were not straight yet. At the same time I was too afraid of being alone with him to continue with the appointments. Finally after a lot of frantic thinking, I came upon a solution of sorts. I would make sure that I was never alone with Dr. Omar again by insisting that my mother or father come with me to his office. I was pleased with myself for coming up with this plan, except that I had an awful time convincing my parents to accompany me. They kept saying they didn't have time to come with me to every appointment and why on earth did I want them along after all these months of going alone! In desperation I told them that it hurt every time Dr. Omar adjusted my braces and that I need their presence for emotional support. (Not very far from the truth after all.) Finally my argument won them over and they started taking turns accompanying me.

Dr. Omar never commented on their sudden presence. However, he made a point of telling my Father that he was behind in his payments and that he needed to pay him right away for him to finish the work. Then in his usual curt manner, he told me to open my mouth. It might have been my imagination but I definitely felt more physical pain and discomfort that day in addition to my nervousness of being back in that chair where I had been frightened. I also thought that he was pulling the wires in my mouth harder than he ever had or needed to. Despite the discomfort, I felt a crazy sense of victory that I was getting my teeth fixed and protecting myself.

I never saw the pleasant young dental assistant again. He had someone else after a while. I wondered if she had been fired and felt bad for her. I felt regret at not having had the opportunity to thank her for putting her job on the line and rushing in to help me.

The second traumatic incident occurred when I was seventeen and a senior in an all girls high school. My school was situated in an idyllic hamlet of a suburb of Istanbul, on the Asian side of the city facing the

# BRIDGING THE AEGEAN

Black Sea. You had to go up a steep hill to reach the school, but the reward was spectacular views of the Bosphorus.

I'll never forget the day the incident happened. It was an unusually warm afternoon for Spring; early May is usually cool. A group of us Seniors, all boarding students, were playing volleyball in one of the outdoor courts after school hours, taking a break between studying for finals. We were wearing our gym uniforms: navy regulation shorts and white knit tops. I was enjoying the game totally; I have always enjoyed playing volleyball! It was a perfect way to relax and forget all my worries and concerns. While I was on the court, nothing mattered but hitting that ball. It was my turn to serve. My side was winning and there were excited screams from my team urging me to serve well. As I was ready to serve the ball, I saw Professor Ahmet Bey strolling by. This was our esteemed Turkish professor, famous for his formal demeanor and exacting academic standards. His appearance was not imposing: He was a short balding overweight middle aged man and we were all a little afraid of him because he was famous for sharp sarcastic reprimands in class if we did not give him the right answers to his questions.

As I saw him going by on my side of the court, I nodded my head in respectful recognition and mouthed Merhaba (Hello). He stopped, looked at me, and quickly uttered a vulgar sexual expression about wanting to perform a sexual act on me. He said all this in perfect Greek, so I was the only one who understood the words being the only Greek on the courts that day. I was so shocked at what I heard that I refused to believe my ears. My immediate thought was that I had misunderstood him or that he didn't know what he was saying. I had not even known that he spoke Greek, few Turks did; and I had always conversed with him in Turkish. I stood there holding the ball, shocked to the core, unable to lift my arms to serve. My team was yelling at me to play, but I felt too paralyzed to move. Finally in robot-like motion, I served a dud ball. From the corner of my eye I saw Ahmed Bey looking at me and winking. I started realizing there had been no misunderstanding after all. Most probably he did say the sexual vulgarity and addressed it to me.

The joy and innocence of that afternoon game evaporated in an instant. By the mores of the Greek community I was a very young and sheltered seventeen-year-old. Not only had I no sexual experience, but I had not even been on a date alone with a guy. I did not know the terms "sexual harassment" or "verbal sexual abuse" back then, but I did not have to know the words to experience the feelings and the crushing effect of Ahmet Bey's behavior.

The rest of the afternoon and evening was a blur. I could not concentrate on studying or anything else. My sleep was very fretful that evening. I kept tossing and turning, trying to figure out what I was going to do. I had the "esteemed" professor in two classes every week; and even though school was almost out for the year, I knew that I would have him as a teacher in college for the next four years. How could I go back to his classroom and pretend that everything was normal? Could I be that good at acting? I had always been told by my family and friends that I had a transparent face that showed all my feelings. Well, now, for the first time in my life I had to wear a mask to hide my feelings. I never considered telling anybody. Who could I tell? My Mother, who had always been extremely protective of me, would have been furious at my teacher's behavior; and I had no doubt that she would have stormed into the school, created a big scene, and probably made it harder for me to graduate from high school and move on to college—or so I thought. Would the school authorities believe me? I strongly doubted that. It would have been my word against a respected member of the faculty. After all, Ahmet Bey was an icon of respectability in the academic community, with a wife and five kids and a long illustrious record as a senior Turkish faculty member.

I truly believe that the cards were stacked against me anyway. The Principal of our school, for reasons that I never understood, made it clear on numerous occasions that she did not like me, even though I was a very good student and did not misbehave. Early on in high school she had accused me of being a liar, a false accusation that had stung, especially since honesty had always been an important value to me. Her contention was that I had learned English "too quickly", and so according to her faulty logic, I must have lied to her upon admission to the school when I told her I didn't speak the language. My protestations were to no avail. I pointed out to her that I already spoke Greek, Turkish and French and maybe those other languages had helped me learn English more quickly. She never seemed to believe me and went out of her way to scold me on any occasion she could. I couldn't wait to graduate from high school and move on to the college level so as to get away from her bias towards me.

Looking back, I remember a plain, obese, unhappy-looking woman who wore shapeless dresses with her gray hair in a bun, and no makeup, with a mustache. She brought gloom and negativity to every gathering that she attended. Given all this, I knew with certainty that I could not go to her to complain about the sexual remark. With a history between us, my fear was that she would laugh at me or treat me with disdain and not only take the professor's side, but accuse me of spreading vicious lies. By morning I came to the conclusion that I had to keep the incident a secret and act as if nothing had happened. I did not even tell my close friends about what happened, afraid that somehow they would tell others and it would come back to hurt me.

So I kept the silence once again just like I did when I was fourteen years old, and attended Ahmet Bey's class for four more years. I never entered his classroom without a feeling of dread and fear. Often the sinking feeling inside would result in stomach cramps on the days when one of his classes was on my schedule. At times I would minimize the incident in my mind thinking that maybe I did not hear his words correctly or that it wasn't that big a deal. I tried to avoid the professor as much as possible. Since neither of us ever alluded to the incident, after a year or so I came to the point of thinking that maybe I had imagined the whole thing.

# BRIDGING THE AEGEAN

Then my junior year of college arrived and the big annual Spring trip. This was very appealing one for me. My class was to travel by train throughout the Mediterranean region of Turkey and even get to see some of the famous Byzantine ruins of the ancient city of Ephesus that were just being excavated. The trip would also include a visit to Pamukkale, a place with warm spring waters that looked from a distance like a cotton hill, hence the name. After I signed up for the trip and made the necessary deposit, I found out to my dismay that Ahmet Bey was going to be one of the two faculty members going with us on the trip. I got an immediate sinking feeling in my stomach but felt that it was too late to back out. I rationalized to myself that the vulgar sexual remark had been said three years earlier and there had been no repetition or any indication that the incident had even occurred. I told myself not to be a coward and to go on this trip as planned.

It was indeed a wonderful trip. I loved visiting the small Turkish towns along the Mediterranean coast that were more like primitive villages than towns. At that time undeveloped and totally free of tourists, the beaches were practically empty and the turquoise-blue waters of the Aegean Sea, pristine and clear. One of the places that particularly intrigued me was Ephesus, an ancient Greco-Roman city, now visited by thousands of tourists every year, then practically empty except for the international team of archeologists who were busy excavating. Nearly two thousand years ago, this was the busiest harbor of Asia Minor where traders from different parts of the world would gather to sell their merchandise while also paying homage to the goddess Artemis in an imposing temple bearing her name. While we were there, we saw that some of the ruins of the columns of the Library of Celsus had been partially excavated. We marveled at their beauty and durability through the centuries.

One day, as we were walking around the site, I noticed a small stone house standing alone on a hill above the ruins. I asked what it was and was told that it was believed to be the last residence of Mary, the Mother of Jesus. Curious, I walked by myself to the house and saw a tiny sign next to it indicating that she had lived there some years before her death. I had never heard of this house before. I made a mental note to myself to tell my religious Mother about it, knowing she would be very moved by my discovery. Unfortunately, I could not go inside the house because there was a big lock on the door and a sign that said that it was off limits. Little did I know then that that modest house would one day attract millions of visitors including two Popes!

Not far from Ephesus we came to the enchanting site of Pamukkale. I gasped when I first saw it. A waterfall tumbled over layers of limestone and gave the appearance of pristine snow. There were pools of water formed all around the side like little lakes shimmering in the sunlight. It is named Pamukkale ("cotton hill" in Turkish) because from a distance it resembles a hill of cotton. It is fed by a mineral rich, fresh water spring and was radiantly beautiful. The ancient Romans built a thermal spa around the spring and would boast of its healing powers. Our trip was in late April and even though at that time of the year it's still much too cool to swim in the Mediterranean Sea, it was different here in the geological wonder of Pamukkale. We hurriedly put on our bathing suits, took some dips in small pools, and quickly discovered that the spring fed water was nice and warm as a cocoon. We understood then what the Romans were boasting about. We were all quite reluctant to leave magical Pamukkale and continue on our journey.

After a week on the trip, some of my earlier trepidation of being in the same train quarters as Ahmet Bey was lifted. My classmates kept commenting on how nice he was and how relaxed and friendly outside the classroom. I kept my mouth shut about the incident of three years ago and did not contradict them. I did make some effort to never be alone with him.

Since there were inadequate sleeping facilities outside the big cities at the time (The year was 1955 and tourists had not yet discovered Turkey) a decision had been made by school authorities that we would all sleep on the train. The last night before our return to Istanbul, I was thinking to myself that I would miss the girls and the lovely Mediterranean vistas. It was rather late, around 11:00 PM and most of the girls were asleep. As was my usual routine before bedtime I had been reading an exciting book and had not wanted to stop. I put on a robe on top of my nightgown and went to use the small washroom before going to sleep. I noticed there was very little light in the passageway and so I was walking slowly so as not to fall since the train was moving. As I neared the washroom, I saw the dim light of a cigarette coming from a shadowy figure in the corner. Alarmed, I jumped up and drew back. It was Ahmet Bey. "Don't be scared," he said in perfect Greek as he touched my arm. "It's only me. And you're still as pretty as ever, especially in your nightgown, and I'm still interested in doing to you what I suggested three years ago on the volley ball court." I was speechless. My heart was beating like crazy and I ran back to my compartment, forgetting all about the washroom. I huddled in my bed and drew up my covers to my chin, trembling like a leaf. The train that had been my happy home in the last two weeks seemed all of a sudden terribly unsafe and I felt scared and vulnerable. I kept seeing shadows in all the dark corners of my compartment.

Now I knew with certainty that the sexual harassment incident of three years ago had really happened and was exactly as my shocked mind had understood it before denial stepped in and made me doubt my hearing and understanding. I didn't sleep at all that night. I was greatly relieved to see my Mother's face the next day at the train station as she waited for me with the other parents. Again true to form I did not say a word about what happened on the train the previous night. I told my Mother that it was a wonderful trip and that I had a great time touring the Mediterranean part of Turkey—a mostly true statement, at least it was till the last evening and my encounter with our "esteemed" Turkish professor.

Looking back I wonder about his gall and the risk he took in sexually harassing me twice. Didn't he wonder about the possible scandal that could have ensued if I had spoken and had addressed the issue with any authority figure? And what about his reputation in the community, his faculty position and family ties? Did he even stay awake at night worrying that I might expose him? Or did he sleep untroubled and undisturbed, guessing that a young female student, especially a minority one, would not speak up and/or be believed by authority figures even if she did? It angers and pains me to think that he had pegged me rightly that I would keep quiet.

When classes started again after the Spring break, I dreaded more than ever going back to Ahmet Bey's classes. I would try to go inside the classroom as quietly as I could and try to sneak to the back of the room without looking at him. There was always a sinking feeling in my gut as I entered the room; the feeling stayed there throughout the hour. My efforts to go unnoticed would not be very successful. Inevitably, he would call on me and ask me about the day's assignment. Even though I would study and prepare more than usual for his classes, my distress would make me flustered and I would make mistakes here and there despite the fact that almost always I knew the answers to the questions he asked. Then the bastard would ridicule me in front of my classmates and announce that I had not prepared well for his class. He would add with a smirk, "Where is your head? Thinking about boys, no doubt", my classmates would laugh on cue, while I would slump in my seat practically in tears.

One day after he went through his regular routine with me, the class broke up and I fled outside, too embarrassed to talk to any of the other girls. The only other Greek girl in the class, Thalia, approached me in the hallway and asked me if I was OK. She added, "I noticed that our professor has been picking on you a lot lately. Have you done anything to anger him?" I mumbled something about a volleyball game three years ago, and that he had made an insulting remark to me. I added that he had repeated something similar during the train trip. I left it vague. I was too embarrassed to tell her it was a sexual remark both times. She got a knowing look in her eyes and said, "Try not to let him get to you. I have heard rumors to the effect that despite the strict and formal exterior and the five kids, that he's quite a lady's man and that his wife tolerates his behavior so as not to lose her position in the community. His reputation is one big reason I did not come with you on the Spring Trip with the class. I did not want to be in close quarters with that man!" I stared at her, vastly surprised. I had not heard any of the rumors. This was all news to me. She added, "We have to be strong, Froso and remember our heritage. He's needling you and treating you unfairly, partially because you are a Greek girl and he knows he can get away with it. Don't let him see that he has the power to upset you. Do well in the exams like I know you can and he'll have to give you a good grade."

I hugged her and thanked her for her kind words. I wish I could have told her the whole story, but even the partial telling and her response had given me some comfort. My exams were flawless and Ahmet Bey gave me an "A" for the exam. However, my final grade for his class was a "B". I gathered up my courage and went to his office to ask why I had a

# BRIDGING THE AEGEAN

"B" instead of an "A". He said, "Your oral responses in my classes were not up to par. You're darn lucky I gave you a "B". Good bye." I cried as soon as I left his office; I didn't want him to see me crying. I thought of going to the Dean of the school, but then I remembered that as a senior I would have him for another year. And I was also afraid that in my emotional state the truth would come out, I would have a fight on my hands, and possibly endanger my college degree. So I did nothing about the grade and cried myself to sleep that night.

Without Ahmet Bey in my life, the summers of my adolescence were a lot more carefree and pleasant. Almost all of them were spent in *Burgaz* Island, about an hour's distance from Istanbul by ferryboat. One summer when I was eighteen and a recent high school graduate, my Mother, Stepfather and I were renting the bottom half of a two-story cottage on top of a hill in the island. It was better than most of the cottages we usually rented in the summer. As long as there was running water and electricity, my Mother was satisfied. I was particularly delighted that if I looked straight ahead from a certain spot on the long deck in front of our family room I could even see a small view of the turquoise water of the Sea of Marmara, a rare luxury for mid-range rentals in the island.

Our landlord lived above us on the top level. Since he had a separate door from which he came and went, we hardly saw the man. All we knew about him was that he was Turkish and a retired sea captain. We heard our neighbors address him in a respectful manner as "Kapetan

## Froso Hacipara Sendukas

Bey" (Mr. Captain). Whenever we crossed paths—which was a rare occurrence—he would greet us in a formal manner and then without any small talk, he would proceed to his own quarters. My Mother and Stepfather thought of him as "a perfect gentleman."

About two months after we moved in (We would usually spend three months in the island) he introduced us to a young woman and told us she was his niece, Ayla, from Ankara, capital of Turkey, who had arrived to spend some time with him. She seemed very shy and reserved, but she was about my age and it didn't take us long before she and I became rather friendly. I did notice that she would only seek my company when her uncle was absent from the house. She was vague about her personal history but she did tell me that our landlord helped financially support her family and that she was grateful to him for that. After a while, she let it slip that she wasn't particularly happy in Burgaz, away from home. She blushed as she said this, but implied that there was a certain young man in Ankara whom she liked and did not want to be parted from. However, her family did not approve of him as a prospective husband for her, hence the trip to Burgaz to spend a month with her uncle. Ayla, being a product of a traditional Muslim family, would not dare go against their wishes. With a sad look in her face, she told me that her family would probably arrange a marriage soon to someone a lot older than her, who they considered more appropriate. She made me promise not to say a word about all this to anyone, especially her uncle.

One early evening after dinner she and I were sitting in my favorite corner of the deck looking at the water and talking. It was a lovely

# BRIDGING THE AEGEAN

August evening with a gentle breeze making the warm temperature of the day more temperate. This was a rare occasion since we never spent time together in the evenings when her uncle was present. As we were chatting away, all of a sudden I saw Kapetan Bey approach. Ayla immediately froze when she saw her uncle and rose from her seat to go greet him. I saw the fear in her eyes that he would scold her for being with me. However, the captain was in a rare jovial mood and he surprised us both by greeting me warmly and suggested that the three of us take a stroll in this lovely summer evening. I saw Ayla imploring me with her eyes to say, "Yes." So I did and we went for our walk.

It was a pleasant walk at first, even though I did not much like the Captain. I resented the fact that he held his niece practically a prisoner in his house and would not allow her to go anywhere with me or with anybody else. The evening stroll turned out to be a very long walk. As the Captain led us toward a grove of trees, I heard Ayla say timidly in Turkish, "Uncle, it's getting very dark and I'm tired. Maybe we should start going back to the house." He turned to her and said, "Why don't you go home! Froso and I will follow shortly." He then gave her a little shove and she started walking away. I said, uneasy about the sudden development, "Maybe we should go back too. It is late and my Mother will worry." He said, "Didn't you tell us earlier that your Mother and Stepfather were playing cards at a friend's house? I doubt that they'll be home yet." I looked around and realized we were all alone in the middle of a dark forest. My uneasiness grew and I said, "I think I'll go back anyway and join Ayla." He grabbed me by the shoulders and said,

"You're not going anywhere yet, not before you give me a little sample of your charms," and started kissing me. I smelled alcohol on his breath and tried to get away from the unwelcome embrace, but he was holding me so tight I thought I would suffocate. At this point I thought how stupid I was for going along on this walk. I struggled and screamed, "Hayir" (No!), but I knew that it was hopeless to struggle; the place was totally isolated. I knew that no one would hear me. Just then, Ayla appeared out of nowhere and her Uncle loosened his grip on me and let me go. "I heard a scream," she said. "Are you all right, Froso?" The Captain had a furious look on his face. "You were supposed to go home, idiot girl," he said. "What on earth are you doing back here?" I saw her trembling; I didn't wait to hear her reply. I ran home as fast as I could and locked myself in the house till my parents came home. Once again an older man, who seemed so proper and formal at first took advantage of my vulnerability and naiveté and became a sexual aggressor. Once again a young woman had rescued me at her own risk.

The next day I waited till I saw the Captain leave the house and then I went and knocked on Ayla's door. I could hear the sounds of crying coming from inside the room. It added to my worrying about the consequences of her rescuing efforts the night before. She opened the door and I gasped! I saw ugly bruises on her face and arms and I was appalled. "Did he hit you?" I asked. She nodded and cried even harder. I hugged her and told her how sorry I was that she had been beaten, and that she had been heroic last night. I added that I would always be grateful to her. "I hope you return to your family in Ankara immediately," I said, "and not subject yourself to your Uncle's violent behavior." She kept sobbing and telling me that she couldn't go back home. "They won't believe me," she said. They'll punish me even more for lying. Plus remember he supports us financially, so they would never want to antagonize him." I begged her to let me call her family and explain to them what happened. Maybe they would believe me. She shook her head, "No". "There's some things you don't know about me or my family," she said between sobs. "My Uncle has been molesting me for years. I tried early on to tell my Mother and she said that her Brother would never do such a thing; that he was an honorable gentleman and forbade me from ever mentioning it again or telling my Father. So you see I can't go back to my family or tell them what happened. You mustn't tell them either." I stood there looking at my young friend, terribly sorry for her and powerless to help her.

Even though Ayla had asked me not to tell, I was so outraged by the Captain's treatment of his niece that I told my Mother about her bruises and my concern about her. I did not mention the sexual abuse nor did I tell her about the sexual aggression towards me the night before. My Mother—even without knowing the whole story read between the lines and told me that she was shocked and she would talk with the Captain right away

I never saw Ayla again. I was told by my Mother that she had gone back to her family in Ankara and that the Captain had told her that it was a family affair and not to worry about his niece. Since Ayla had given me no address in Ankara, I did not know how to communicate with her. I wanted to believe that she told her family the truth one more time and that maybe her bruises would make them believe her and not send her anymore to spend time with her abusive Uncle. I would like to believe all that but I have no way of knowing. My Mother would never rent from her Uncle ever again and I never saw him again even though we returned to the island every summer. I'll always remember brave sweet Ayla and what she did for a Greek girl whom she barely knew.

# BRIDGING THE AEGEAN

## THE SYMBOL OF VIRGINITY

In some countries it is prized more than rubies. In others (i.e., Denmark, Sweden, U.K. and the U.S.), the general assumption seems to be that it is not to be expected. I'm talking about virginity, "young women's virginity" to be exact. Nobody seems to care about whether men are virginal or not—except perhaps the men themselves, who for the most part cannot wait to shed the burdensome mantle of virginity!

I noticed recently (2009) that the subject of virginity was in the news again. It was a small item, half buried in our local Houston newspaper. The title of the article was "Ban urged on fake virginity tests".

It seems that in Cairo, Egypt, lawmakers had called for a ban on imports of a Chinese—made kit meant to help young women fake their virginity. The "artificial virginity hymen" kit costs $30.00 and is intended to help newly married women fool their husbands into believing that they are still virgins!

Egypt, being a country with Middle Eastern morals and ancient cultural beliefs that refuse to die (like many other countries, especially in the Middle East) considers a woman valuable as a bride only if her virginity is intact. Hence the import and marketing of the above product. It seems that the fake virginity kit leaks a blood like substance when opened.

My first reaction the above news bulletin was laughter. The idea behind the kit struck me as so outrageous and ridiculous that I couldn't believe that anybody would produce it and sell it, let alone buy it. But then, after the laughter, came a very different reaction. I started feeling sad and angry on behalf of all the young women all over the world who were still treated as a commodity and whose value as human beings increased or decreased according to the "virginal" status!

My angry feelings were mostly directed at societies who with parents of daughters as accomplices, kept the unfair cultural double standard going, the sad feelings were for the intended brides who did not have a choice in the matter as to how they were treated and how their value was calculated.

What about rape victims, I thought statistics and tragic news events tell us time and time again that most victims—by far—are female. They get traumatized and victimized twice—once by the violence of the rape act itself and later by the stigma of being raped as well as the lessoning of their value and/or rejection in the marriage market.

As I'm writing this, I'm remembering another news item, also of recent vintage, that made me cry when I read it. This involved an 11 year old girl, somewhere in the U.S., raped by a neighborhood gang. She later walked to a nearby police station, crying and asking for help. When the police called the poor child's family, asking them to come to the police station to pick-up their daughter and take her home, the girl's newly immigrant father told the police that his daughter was no longer welcome at her home because of what happened to her. She was now "damaged goods"!

I'm not a violent person, but when I read the above news story, I remember feeling rage inside. I felt the urge to go find this man and shake him till his bones rattled!

I would like to believe that I would have been enraged by the above events even if I did not have a personal experience to relate it to. The truth is that I *did* lose the symbol of virginity at age 12 but that momentous experience had nothing to do with sex—violent or otherwise. In fact it happened in the presence of my mother, my aunt and two family friends. We were on a sailboat that day, close to the island of Burgaz (1-½ hours by ferryboat from Istanbul) where my family and I spent most summers, renting a cottage for the season. The sailboat belonged to a couple who were close family friends. They had invited us to spend part of the day with them by going sailing. I have always loved being on a sailboat and gently cruising the lovely turquoise–blue waters of the Sea of Marmara, so I was excited by the invitation.

I vividly remember that particular day in September even though it happened more than 50 years ago. The weather was perfect—it was warm without being hot with low humidity and a light breeze moving the sails of the boat in a rhythmic pattern and sound that was music to my ears. I was lying on the lower part of the boat—as was my habit—mellow and half asleep, hypnotized by the gentle movement and sounds of the sails when I suddenly realized that something had changed. The boat was swaying and the sails were moving back and forth but the rhythm was not gentle anymore. The weather had abruptly changed and the tranquil sea had lost its tranquility. The light breeze had become a strong wind and the sea around us was turning grey and dark-blue instead of shimmering turquoise. I sat up and realized that I was having a hard time hanging on to my balance and not falling.

At first, we all stayed calm. After all, the owner of the boat was an experienced amateur sailor and everybody in this excursion group knew how to swim. I did notice though that our friend more and more seemed to have a hard time controlling the sails. I was also becoming aware that I was feeling chilled in my bathing suit. I knew that I had brought a sweater with me, so I started looking for my beach bag. I noticed that the bag was on the other side of the boat and I started moving towards the bag. Suddenly, a strong gust of wind changed the direction of the sails and the boat lurched forward. I immediately lost my balance and sat or rather fell on top of the mast. I instantly felt a searing, intense pain and I screamed. Everybody froze and looked at me. As if in a haze, I saw my mother run to my side and try to pick me up. The pain was so severe that I felt glued to the mast—I could not move—even with my mother's help—I heard her say "Frosula, Frosula" and something else, but I could not hear or understand the rest. I felt a warm liquid running down my thighs and legs and realized to my horror that I was bleeding profusely and that my blood was staining both my suit and the boat. Being in shock, I could not find out where the blood was coming from. I did not see any cuts on my legs or thighs and somehow, not figuring out the source of the blood—I was panicking. "Mama", I yelled, "Where is the blood coming from? Am I dying?" My mother took one look at the blood and fainted. I don't remember anything else of the day. My aunt who was on the boat also told me later that I had fainted as well!

When I regained my consciousness, I found myself lying on a slat—that took the place of a bed—with a man in a white uniform bending over me looking concerned. I asked him where I was and he told me that I was in the one and only Medical Clinic in the island, run by the Turkish "Red Cross", I had never been in this clinic. My mother used to tell me that it was a joke and not worth much. So in the rare occasions that I would get sick in the summer—she would take me to a doctor in Istanbul. Right now, since I was still in pain, I did not care about any of the above. All I wanted was some relief from the pain, and all I could do was cry and moan.

The man in uniform told me that they were going to transfer me to a hospital in Istanbul as soon as the special "Red Cross" ferry boat arrived. I had never heard of this special ferry boat but I was glad of its existence. From the corner of my half closed eyes, I saw my mother holding my hand, looking as pale as a ghost. I must have fainted again because I have no recollection of the transfer to the special ferry boat

nor to the Medical Center in Istanbul. Next thing that happened that I was aware of was hearing my mother say, "Don't worry, Frosula, first thing tomorrow morning I am taking you to the Italian hospital to see Dr. Violi. He will treat you and you will be fine, I promise!" And then she leaned towards me and whispered—"I don't trust this Medical Center and you know how much faith I have in Dr. Violi's skills." Boy did I know! (Dr. Violi was a doctor in Istanbul of Italian descent that my mother idolized. He was a heart surgeon by profession, but my mother did not let his medical specialty get in the way. It did not matter what ailment I or anybody else in the family had—mother's first step was always to take us to Dr. Violi and hear what he had to say.
I gathered from what she said that, this being a Sunday, that Dr. Violi was not available to see me.

Next morning bright and early we went to see her superhero. Dr. Violi was a gentle man with a beard and a calming demeanor. Since my mother trusted him implicitly, I did not mind going to see him—not that I had much choice.

After the doctor examined me, he took my mother aside and started talking to her in a hushed tone. His behavior gave me another scare. Did I have such a serious injury that he wouldn't even let me hear what he was saying? On previous visits to his office, he had always been forthright and honest in telling me and my mother what he thought was wrong with me—and I had always liked that about him. So why was he acting in the furtive, secretive manner? I started getting quite suspicious about my injury. After we left the doctor's office, I was even afraid to ask my mother about what they had whispered about.

That evening, as I was going to bed, I couldn't stand the "mystery" anymore, so I turned to her and said, "What's going on, Mama, is there something about my boat accident that you're not telling me? Why was Dr. Violi whispering to you in private? That's not like him!"

My mother stroked my hair and said, "*Pethi mu* (my child), you are right to be upset. I *am* keeping something from you. I was waiting for the right moment to tell you. "Remember, when you fell in Uncle Mihali's boat how much it hurt?" "How can I forget?" I replied. "It hurt a lot, and there was blood running down my legs, and I couldn't tell where it was coming from."

My mother let out a loud sigh. "I'm glad that you are so innocent that you don't know certain things," she said, "Do you know, Frosula, how people can tell if a girl is a virgin?" I shrugged my shoulders. I had no idea how to answer her question and I was perplexed about the turn the conversation had taken. At age 12 worrying about virginity and/or the lack of it was not an important concern.

Growing up as I had in Turkey's Greek community, I knew that I would not be allowed to date during my teenage years, or even later. Dating was for the girls of "Seventeen" magazine in far away U.S.A., not for the likes of me. At the same time, I knew with certainty that safeguarding one's virginity was very important in my world.

My mother did not have to admonish me or lecture me about the *value* of virginity, the critical comments that I had overheard through the years about "fallen" girls made it very clear to me how the Greeks of "Stin Poli" (Istanbul) viewed the girls who made the tenable mistake of having a baby out of wedlock—defying the values of our society came with a hefty price. They were shamed and shunned—their reputation and respectability gone forever!

As these thoughts were going through my head, I noticed that my mother had not spoken for a while and had a sad expression on her face. I said—"Mama, what are still hiding from me? What are you *not* telling me?" In a tearful voice she whispered something about a "torn membrane". "What are you talking about?" I asked, "What torn membrane?" By now, I was totally confused by the turn that our conversation had taken. "When you had your boat accident," my mother construed, "your vaginal membrane was shed through and torn by your fall on top of the mast. That's why you hurt so much and that's why you were bleeding."

"So what!" I replied, immensely relieved that I was not dying. "It must have healed by now, right?"

"No," she said softly. When the hymen—that's what the vaginal membrane is called—is torn, Frosula, it does not grow back to its original state."

"And?" I asked, still not understanding why my mother was making such a big deal about his, "the pain is mostly gone, so why are you so upset by this, Mama?"

My mother let out a big sigh, "Frosula, I am glad that age 12 you're still so innocent about sexual matters, but I have to tell you something important, pethi mu. You see, your unfortunate boat accident with its consequence of the torn hymen destroyed the evidence of your being a virgin, that's why I have been so upset. Let us hope that your future husband—whoever he may be—will be an understanding and trusting man and will be satisfied with your explanation of what happened.

"Of course he will" I said. "I promise you mama that I will marry a nice man who not only will not care about this silly thing called "hymen", but will absolutely believe anything that I tell him. By the way, mama, "do men have a similar membrane?" My mother laughed as she replied, "not that kind of membrane, Frosula!" The truth is nobody cares if men are virgins or not when they marry. All society cares about is whether the girls are virgins. "That's not fair," I said, and walked away, glad to have this embarrassing conversation over with.

## Froso Hacipara Sendukas

Moving fast forward to ten years later, here I was—now 22 years old—and a new resident of U.S. on my wedding night in Louisiana—a long way from my family and home in Istanbul. My husband and I had dated back home for four years. He left Turkey in 1955 to continue his studies in America—after I graduated from the American College in Istanbul in 1956, I joined him in Baton Rouge, Louisiana where he had just started a job with the Highway Department.

So here we were on our wedding night. Amidst the numerous mixed emotions I was feeling - anticipation, glee as well as some anxiety and homesickness (during the wedding ceremony, attended by only a few newly formed friends, I had acutely missed the presence of my family and lifelong friends). Who knew if I would ever see them again - - . I tried to shake off the gloomy thoughts and concentrate on the present. As I thought of my mother and how happy she would have been to see me getting married, I remembered our long-ago conversation about virginity.

"Honey, I said as my groom was embracing me, wait first a second. This is not a big deal but I have something to tell you." "Can't this wait till later?", he asked, visibly annoyed at the interruption. "No," I replied, "I think I need to tell you now." I proceeded to tell him about my boat accident of ten years ago, fully expecting him to laugh it off. He did not. His arms, that had been encircling me till then, dropped to his sides, and he said, "A likely story!" I froze. His reaction was certainly not what I expected or had thought I would hear.

# BRIDGING THE AEGEAN

He must have seen the stricken expression on my face because he quickly said, "I'm kidding, I'm kidding, don't take things so seriously!"

I looked at him and reminded myself that this was the man that I had waited for 5 years to marry and had crossed many oceans and lands so as to be by his side, leaving family and friends behind. So I chose to believe at that moment that he was joking even though a voice inside me was telling me otherwise. Nice girls from where I was did <u>not</u> question their husbands nor flee on the eve of their future and throw away their dreams on the basis of disappointed expectations and a few insensitive words.

After all, I had burned my bridges and had left my old life behind to come to this exciting new country. So, I forced a smile on my face and did not ever say another word on the subject of virginity—mine or anybody else's.

The thought that came to me later was: "You can take the person out of the Middle East, but can you take the Middle East out of the person?"

Froso Hacipara Sendukas

# BRIDGING THE AEGEAN

## THE LAST TRIP

Mother's last trip to the United States was in 1974, when I graduated from the University of Houston's School of Social Work with a master's degree

She had insisted on coming to the ceremony all the way from Turkey despite the fact that her health had been recently failing. She had a heart attack the previous year and had not told me about it til many months later. She confessed at the time that her doctors had told her to quit smoking "or else…"

She quit for a month, then went back to it. Unfortunately, the addiction was stronger than dire medical warnings.

I went with my whole family to pick her up at the airport. As I saw her exiting the plane, my heart sank. Her complexion was very pale and she looked quite frail. She saw us through the glass double doors of the airport's waiting area and tried to smile but I could tell that it was a forced, strained smile. I told myself that she was probably just tired from the long flight, but deep down I knew differently.

When I thanked her for coming to my graduation she smiled and said, "I am the one who needs to thank you, Frosula, you have surpassed my goals for you. I never dreamed you would go back to school after having three children and that you would earn an advanced degree. Remember what I used to always tell you about higher education?"

I smiled and said, "I sure do!" and I quoted her, saying: "For a woman, a college education is more valuable than a diamond bracelet!" We shared a laugh.

She asked me if I knew what I wanted to do with my degree. I told her about my internship during the second year of graduate school and how inspiring it had been.

"My placement was at TRIMS (Texas Research Institute for Mental Sciences, now closed). Individuals and families could get outpatient psychiatric care based on a sliding fee scale. I worked with two families there. And with my supervisor I co-led a group of schizophrenic patients, helping them function on their own in the outside world. The experience was scary at first, but later, when I saw some positive results, turned out to be stimulating and even exciting. That's when I decided, Mama, to be a psychotherapist and help people overcome their mental health problems. I can't wait to get started! I just know I'm going to love doing this."

My mother 's eyes shone as she listened to me. "Was the place where you studied anything like Balukli?" she asked.

I was suddenly flooded with memories. During my childhood years, my mother would regularly visit orphanages and hospitals and volunteer to help out. One of the places she frequently visited was a Greek hospital and geriatric facility named "Balukli." It also had a psychiatric section and that's where Mother would spend most of her time. Knowing her childhood history, I understood about her interest in orphans, but I couldn't figure out why she would expose herself to "crazy" people (as I would call the patients in my head, but not in her presence).

Once in a while she would take me along on her charitable visits, or more accurately, drag me along. I didn't mind visiting the orphanages even though the clingy neediness of the children would sadden me and make me feel vaguely guilty. But I just hated going to Balukli, especially the psychiatric center. I thought that the patients of the facility were really "weird." (Years later when I saw the movie One Flew Over the Cuckoo's Nest, some of the scenes looked quite familiar.) The psychiatric patients at Balukli would alarm me (powerful psychotic drugs had not been invented yet). It would scare me to see grown men and women screaming and fighting with each other and/or huddling in a corner sobbing. Unlike me, Mother did not seem scared by the patients' antics. She would calmly circulate among them in the big meeting room, distributing Greek goodies like baklava and halva, as well as cigarettes, which were not known then as a health hazard.

The patients, some of whom obviously remembered her from previous visits, would shout, "Madame Anastasia, please don't forget me! Some candy and cigarettes, please!" After Mother would give them what she had brought, some of the patients would try to kiss her hands, thanking her. Then Mother could cry. Once in a while, thankfully not often, she would run out of offerings, and that's when a few of them would get angry and scream at her. The staff would come to the rescue, stepping in, telling us it was time to leave.

Self-centered young girl that I was, especially during my teenage years, I would get very irritated at my mother for pulling me into when I then considered a perilous situation. Instead of admitting the truth, that I was scared, I would say angry things to her. One day, after listening to any ugly outburst from a patient, I remember turning to Mother and asking her, "Why on Earth don't you just send the hospital some money, like 'normal' people? Why do you have to come and be insulted or yelled at? Haven't you noticed that the patients never seem to get any better?" I saw some of the same patients every visit. What was the point of her going?

After my outburst I saw sadness in my mother's eyes and I felt some twinges of guilt about my insensitivity. Maybe I had overreacted to the situation. Mother was silent for a long time and I was afraid I had gone too far with my comments. Had I hurt her too deeply?

Finally she said, "I'm very sorry that the visits to this place are upsetting you so, Frosula. You don't have to come back any more. I'm doing this in memory of my father, Krionas, the grandfather you never met. Maybe if he had not felt so alone and helpless, dealing with his terrible 'melancholia,' he might not have killed himself or place himself in the position to be killed by the Turkish authorities. Don't you see, Frosula, just sending money would not achieve the same purpose. It's just not the same thing. The patients need to know that somebody cares, that they are not forgotten. Do you understand what I'm saying?"

Yes, I did understand, sort of. After that day, I never again complained about our visits to the psychiatric hospital even thought I still dreaded them.

On my graduation day I shared some of my Balukli memories with my mother and thanked her for taking me along on her charity visits, despite my being a "pain in the neck" with my constant complaints and sulking demeanor. Also I told her that our long-ago talk about the reason for visiting Balukli must have had a much deeper impact on me than I had realized.

She hugged me and said, "I'm so happy and so proud that you want to help the mentally ill. Your grandfather, Krionas, must surely be smiling up in Heaven!"

Froso Hacipara Sendukas

# BRIDGING THE AEGEAN

## BLACK SKIN

My mother came from Turkey to stay with my then-husband and me when I was eight months pregnant with my first child. This was her first visit to the United States and she found life here full of wonders. She spent her time alternating between worrying about my condition and wanting to go to department stores to buy all the required presents on her list. She followed the same routine on all her subsequent trips to the US, till I put my foot down years later and told her I was not driving her all over town to buy presents for the neighborhood grocer, the butcher, and a multitude of friends and neighbors. "But I promised," she would say when I'd protest; to mother, a promise was sacred and could not be broken.

One episode that I still remember vividly from that first visit took place in the downtown section of Alexandria, Louisiana where I was living at the time. The year was 1958. This was the era of Civil Rights activities. There was a lot of tension in the air and some dramatic confrontations between "Negroes" (as African-Americans were called publicly back then; "Niggers", as many Southerners called them behind their backs), and the police in public places.

I also remember billboards around town with a picture of Martin Luther King Jr. and the words: "Beware of this man! The head of the FBI, J. Edgar Hoover, says he is a Communist tool and a threat to our country".

## Froso Hacipara Sendukas

Having arrived in the US from Istanbul, Turkey just a couple of years earlier, I was astounded and saddened by the depth of negative racial feelings in my newly adopted country. I was appalled by the hateful comments I was hearing about the attempts of some black activists to integrate Alexandria, Louisiana. Even my neighbors, who at first seemed like nice people, would bristle when I would say that maybe integration did not have to be such a terrible word. Immediately they would put me in my place by telling me that I was a "foreigner" and thus not equipped to understand their situation and the dire consequences that mixing of the races would bring to the South and especially our town.

I would hear these comments and despair about life in the US. Having been a member of a minority group till only recently, my sympathies were definitely with the Civil Rights Movement. The only antidote that I had to the poison around me was my subscription to Time magazine. I would eagerly read the magazine each week from cover to cover. The articles and letters to the editors would give me some hope about living in this country and bringing up my children here.

This was the atmosphere in Alexandria when my mother arrived for her first visit in September 1958. Since I did not drive yet we took a couple of buses and went downtown to shop. Mother exclaimed about all the wonderful clothes she was seeing at the stores. Then we started walking; I was hot and tired. Not only was I eight months pregnant, but the temperature was in the high 90s. I started looking for an air conditioned coffee shop so we could get out of the heat and humidity.

# BRIDGING THE AEGEAN

All of a sudden I noticed that Mother was no longer by my side. I looked around and saw her approaching a group of black people, and getting as close to them as she could. To my astonishment I noticed that she was trying to rub herself against them, hoping that she wouldn't be noticed. I also noticed that they were eyeing her suspiciously and trying to step away from her. "What are you doing, Mama?" I said, after calling her to my side. "What do you think I'm doing?" she retorted, "I am trying to touch black skin. Don't you know it's good luck?"

Trying not to laugh, I told her that indeed I did remember the old Greek belief about touching black skin. However, given the times and the town we were in, I told her that her actions could easily be misunderstood. I tried to explain to her about segregation, civil rights, protests in the US, and the ensuing hostile atmosphere, especially in the Deep South and towns like Alexandria, Louisiana. I thought I did a good job of giving her a quick history lesson about contemporary life in the US. She just looked at me with a puzzled expression. "I don't understand," she said, "don't white people here know that it's good luck to touch black skin?" "That's not exactly what they believe, Mama," I said. She shook her head and said, "America is a strange country."

Froso Hacipara Sendukas

# BRIDGING THE AEGEAN

## THE TAXI DRIVER

Even though I was 47 years old when my mother died, with grown children of my own, I still felt like an orphan.

She died suddenly from a heart attack in Istanbul, Turkey, the city of her birth that was always "home" to her. I got the call telling me of her death at 2:00 a.m. My ex-stepfather was the one who called me. "She died quickly", he said, "she didn't suffer and she was not alone."

I was in total shock. Even though Mother had suffered from heart disease for many years and had already had a heart attack ten years earlier, I still did not expect that she would die at age 67. The fact that she was not alone when she died gave me some comfort, since Mother lived alone in her apartment. It was also fitting, I thought, that she was on her way to church when the fatal heart attack occurred. Mother would go to Church on almost every saint's feast day—and since there were hundreds of saints in the Greek Orthodox calendar, this kept her busy throughout the year.

Lost in thought, in a mist of recollection, I became aware once again that my stepfather was still on the phone, still talking to me. "You don't have to travel to Istanbul", he was saying, "it's a long trip. I can sell the furniture and contents of her apartment and send you the proceeds."

## Froso Hacipara Sendukas

The last comment jarred me from my stupor of grief. The idea of strange and apathetic hands and eyes going through my mother's personal belongings was totally unacceptable—even repugnant to me. After all, I was her only child and there were no other surviving members of her family. Her parents were long dead; her only brother, my Uncle Christos was in Greece at the time and in and out of hospitals for various illnesses brought on by many years of alcohol abuse. My mother and stepfather had been divorced for some years and he had remarried. Even though they still worked together and she still had feelings of affection for him, I knew innately that my mother would not have wanted him or his new wife to go through her things.

I told my stepfather in a firm voice to not let anybody touch any of her belongings. I, her beloved daughter, would come to Istanbul and dispose of her belongings. When he protested, saying the landlord wanted the apartment emptied by the end of the month, I asked him to pay another month's rent and I would reimburse him later. Since Mother had lived in that apartment for 36 years (I was there with her for 11 of those years), I figured the landlord owed her at least that much before renting the apartment to somebody else.

So it was arranged that even though I couldn't make it in time for her funeral, that I would arrive in Istanbul in time for *ta saranta*, the Greek Orthodox memorial service that takes place 40 days after a person's death. I was too paralyzed with grief to arrive any sooner.

# BRIDGING THE AEGEAN

I do not remember the plane trip at all. I seem to have been in a fog, totally overwhelmed by sadness and the anticipation of the difficult task awaiting me in Mother's apartment. My sons had volunteered to come with me but I had foolishly turned down their offer, not wanting to disrupt their lives at the time.

The plane landed in Istanbul and for the first time in my life I had a full-fledged panic attack! I sat in my seat while all the other passengers were disembarking and realized that I could not move at all. Finally, as the plane emptied, a KLM stewardess came to my side and said in English, "Miss, this is our final destination. Weren't you going to Istanbul?"

My heart was beating wildly and I felt drenched in sweat. What was going through my head in obsessive fashion was that in the last years of my mother's life, she had told me more than once not to come home after she died. "When I'm gone", she would say, "there's no point in your coming to Istanbul since I will not be able to see you. Stay in America, don't come!" I would tell her not to be morbid. But now, finding myself glued to my seat in the plane, those words of hers were haunting me and I'm sure contributing greatly to the severe anxiety I was feeling. I had this great irrational fear that since I was disobeying her wishes, Mother would be angry with me!

Finally, with the stewardess holding my arm and gently propelling me toward the exit, I limped out of the plane, still feeling disoriented.

## Froso Hacipara Sendukas

As I picked up my luggage from the baggage area, I looked up and saw my stepfather waiting for me outside customs. It was a nice surprise—I did not expect to have anyone waiting for me. We hugged and as I cried on his shoulder, some of the anxiety left me.

I asked that he take me straight to Mother's apartment. I dreaded entering the place where I had spent most of my childhood and early adulthood, and not finding Mother there. I saw, with some relief, that all of Mother's furniture was in its regular place. My stepfather said, "We didn't touch anything, according to your wishes." I whispered tearfully, "Thank you." I told my stepfather that I was ready to go to my hotel and rest, and that I would return to the apartment the next day, by myself, to start sorting out the contents. I was staying in a hotel because I could not bring myself to stay in Mother's apartment, loud with her absence.

My eyes went to the middle of the dining room table; there was my last letter to her and the envelope had been opened. "She got it the day before she died," said my stepfather, "and she told me about it. It made her very happy." I had told her in the letter that I truly appreciated all the love that she had shown me through the years, especially the highest love a parent can show, by letting her only child not only leave home but settle overseas.

## BRIDGING THE AEGEAN

Now that my own children were growing up and leaving home I understood more deeply my mother's sacrifice 25 years ago when she sent me to the United States.

I don't know what had made me write all this in my last letter to her, but I did. And now as I stood looking at the letter through my tears, I had the first comforting, peaceful feeling since I had heard of Mother's death. I understood why I had crossed thousands of miles to come from Houston to Istanbul and Mother's apartment.

I thought I would be all alone for the next few days, but I had underestimated the local communication network. As word spread in town that I was in Mother's apartment daily, I started having visitors. Mother's longtime housekeeper came to see me, as well as some neighbors and friends. I had mixed feelings about these visits. Even though they were time consuming and kept me from my tasks, most were also comforting, especially Mother's friends that were with her when she died. I started getting requests for some of her belongings, being told that Mother had promised them this or that. Since Mother had left no will, it was hard to determine who was telling me the truth and who was not. I did grant some requests and started giving away some of her belongings.

By now, a few of her friends openly criticized me for not having come to Mother's funeral, telling me that since I was her only child, that it had been my dutiful obligation to come. I tried to explain that my grief had been so great that I had not been able to mobilize myself to come earlier. But I doubt they heard or understood what I was trying to tell them; their minds had been made up about what was the "right" thing to do, and that was that. I could hear my mother's voice in my head telling me to ignore the criticism—that this was evidence of narrow-minded thinking. After all, Mother did not even like the traditional Greek custom of close relatives wearing black clothes for months and even years after someone's death. "That's so trivial!" she would say. "What really matters is how one treated the deceased while they were alive—not what color one wore to the funeral or in later months." I thought of Mother's words and I chose to not let the criticism bother me.

One of Mother's closest friends approached me one day and asked me if I wanted to do anything special in her memory. Mother was a generous contributor to various charities, especially the Greek Balukli orphanage. Mother never forgot her own unhappy years in an orphanage—starting at age 9, after her Father died—so she always had a soft spot in her heart for orphaned or unwanted children.

Remembering Mother's history, I asked her friend if we could do something for the orphanage. "Why don't you give them a special dinner, in her memory?" she said, "I'll organize it."

I'll always be grateful to Mother's friend for her suggestion. The dinner event was quite successful (at least the kids from the orphanage seemed happy); and when one of the older children came over to kiss my hand and thank me, I could see, through tearful eyes, my mother's face beaming at me.

One other eventful encounter that happened while I was in Istanbul was with a Turkish taxi driver. Every day for two weeks, I would go back and forth from my hotel to Mother's apartment. Sometimes I would walk back and forth and at other times in Cihangir, her suburb, I would take a taxi.

One rainy day in May, I went to the taxi stand close to her apartment and looked for a taxi. This big, bulky driver approached me and asked me in Turkish, "*Sari hanimin Amerikan kizi mi siniz?*" (Are you the blonde lady's daughter from America?) I was surprised that he knew of her death and my coming to her apartment, and smiled at his appellation of her as "the blonde lady". Mother's wish was she wanted to die a blonde (her natural hair color was brown) and she did. I told him that I was indeed the blonde lady's daughter from America. "Please get in my taxi," he said, "I will take you wherever you want to go at no charge. Your mother was a very nice lady," he added, "she often took my taxi. One day she saw me looking kind of sad and asked me what was wrong. I told her that my wife was quite sick and that I was worried about her. Your mother insisted that I take a break from work and come to her apartment for some hot tea. She also said that she would light a candle for my wife and pray for her health. I thanked her, figuring that God would accept her prayers even if we are Moslem and she is a

## Froso Hacipara Sendukas

Christian woman." He added, "My wife eventually recovered from her illness and I'll never forget your mother's kindness!"

I smiled at him through my tears and thanked him for sharing his story with me. I thought how typical of Mother to reach out to somebody who needed her help.

That's when I knew why I had come to Turkey after her death, even though she had told me not to come. My healing process about her death started that day, during the conversation with the Turkish taxi driver, in my mother's neighborhood.

# BRIDGING THE AEGEAN

## ANASTASIA AND DIMITRI

I have a small black and white photograph of my parents at their wedding. It shows them outside a Greek Orthodox church in Istanbul, Turkey, where they were married. They stand side by side with *stefana* placed on their heads (dried floral wreaths that are an important part of traditional ritual in Greek weddings). Their heads are gently touching and they both have shy smiles on their faces. They make a handsome couple.

Mother is wearing a simple but elegant white wedding gown which she probably designed and sewed herself. She looks very young and vulnerable, she was only 19 years old at the time. She looks quite lovely. Father is wearing a dark-colored simple suit and looks slim and handsome.

There is a big crowd of people standing behind them forming a circle of sorts. I am assuming that these were the guests at their wedding. The bride and groom seem to have eyes only for each other.

I treasure this small wedding picture of my parents because it is the only picture I have of them in the beginning of their joint journey. Every time I look at that sweet picture I am struck by how happy they look even though I never saw them that way.

## Froso Hacipara Sendukas

I have always known that they both had unhappy childhoods. In fact, they had each lost a parent at a young age. Not only that, but neither one received much affection from the remaining parent.

Dimitri, my father, lost his mother after she gave birth to Katina, his younger sister. The children were raised by a stepmother who was, at her best, indifferent to him and was, at her worst, critical and cruel. Dimitri's father, Panayotis, seemed afraid to cross his bossy new wife—even at my young age I could see that. And he was not prone to show affection to his two children. I don't remember my step-grandmother showing any affection toward me, her only grandchild, albeit step-grandchild. I do remember that after she died, Grandfather would ask me to come sit on his lap so that I could show him my favorite doll.

He died when I was 10 years old, and I saw my father deeply grieve the man whose approval he always wanted but rarely received.

Anastasia, my mother, had an even more unhappy childhood. Her father died when she was a child. His death was surrounded by tragic and mysterious circumstances. All she ever knew about his death was that he died while imprisoned by the Turkish army. Her mother, Grandmother Eleni, told her what she herself had been told by the prison authorities: her husband, Krionas, had killed himself in a fit of melancholia, or depression.

# BRIDGING THE AEGEAN

During the small private funeral, a former jail inmate whispered to Eleni that the army story was a cover-up and that Grandfather Krionas had been killed by prison guards. He had been trying to escape!

My nine-year-old mother did not know what to believe. Grandmother Eleni, who found herself a widow at the age of 29, was naturally devastated and would not (or could not) answer any of her daughter's questions then or even later on. Historically speaking, at the time of Grandfather's death there was a war going on and the country was in chaos. In fact, Turkey was not an independent republic at the time. It was part of the vast, though ailing, Ottoman Empire, with Istanbul as its capital city. The year was 1922. Greek and Ottoman armies were struggling for control of the area. England and France were unofficially helping Greece to defeat the Empire ("the sick man of Europe"). The territory was ripe for picking.

The Greeks of Turkey—a Christian minority in an overwhelmingly Muslim country—were, as usual, caught in the middle. My grandparents belonged to this group and lived as citizens under the authority of the Ottoman Empire.

At that time Greece and its European allies had no way of knowing that a charismatic leader, a Turkish general named Mustafa Kemal Pasha, would become the military genius responsible for winning the war and transforming an ailing empire into the Republic of Turkey (1923). A few years later, a grateful nation would give him the title Atatürk ("first

Turk/father of Turks"), after making him the first president of the new nation.

As president, Atatürk brought about some astonishing changes to Mother's homeland. Among other things, he decreed that the government would be based on secular rather than religious laws, that the national alphabet would be Turkish instead of Arabic, and that his fellow citizens would no longer wear religious garb like carsaf (long, black veils and headdresses for women) and fez (iconic red hats for men).

I can only speculate that not everybody in the land was happy about the radical changes, especially Muslim imams and other religious powers that be; but Atatürk was a war hero and he got everything he wanted. Looking back, I'm also speculating that the move away from religiosity in government had to have helped non-Muslim minorities like the Greeks.

My mother, at the young age of nine years, did not understand much of what was going on in the country. All she knew was that her father's death altered the course of her life forever. Once in a while she would tell me about the last time she saw her father, when, with her mother and younger brother, she visited him in the Turkish army jail. "He had deep, sad brown eyes," she would say, "and as he hugged me and kissed me at the end of our visit, he told me not to forget him!" She never saw him again.

## BRIDGING THE AEGEAN

As for Grandmother Eleni, she steadfastly refused to answer any questions about her husband. "I can't talk about him," she would say, even to me, her beloved only grandchild. "I don't know exactly what happened, and it hurts too much to try to figure it out."

I sometimes wondered, through the years, about Krionas, the grandfather I had never known. Not so much about his death but more about his life. How did he wind up in a Turkish army jail? Was he somehow caught up in the war between the Ottomans and Greeks? And since it was evident, even to the prison authorities, that he was suffering from melancholia, why wasn't he in an army hospital getting treatment?

I may never know the answers to these questions, but as they occasionally cross my mind, they trigger a lot of sadness about my grandfather's life, fate, and the effect on my mother's life. Anastasia lost one parent under tragic circumstances and her remaining parent suddenly became physically and emotionally unavailable. To be fair, it is important to note that Grandmother Eleni must have been devastated not only by the loss of her husband, but by being suddenly in the position of a widow with the prospect of having to raise two young children.

How scared she must have been to realize her only tangible asset was a meager education that she had received back in her Anatolian village by the Black Sea. Her mother had taught her some homemaking skills to prepare her for marriage and motherhood, but these were not exactly marketable skills. Her family, still living back in the village during the time of her loss, must have been either unwilling or, more likely, unable to help her in this desperate situation. So, not knowing what else to do, Eleni started cleaning houses and taking in laundry and ironing to support herself and her children.

One of her jobs was to clean buildings at an orphanage run by French Catholic nuns. Somehow the nuns figured out or were told about the young mother's tragedy and they approached her with an offer: lodging and care for her two children in return for her cleaning services. I would like to think she was reluctant to choose this plan. But in the end she agreed to at least a portion of the offer—at the last minute she decided that her five-year-old son, Christo, was too young to live in an orphanage and would stay at home with her. It was because of this decision that my mother, the kindest woman I have ever known, never forgave her own mother.

Grandmother Eleni told Anastasia that since she was nine years old and much more mature than her brother, she could more easily adjust to life at the orphanage and at the same time get a free education and learn the French language. Didn't that make logical sense? Not according to my mother. She never forgot the exact moment when her mother left her at the orphanage. She told me, numerous times through the years, that she felt abandoned and very alone in the world. She still needed nurturing care and affection. From that moment on, Anastasia felt second best in her mother's affections. At this point in her story, Mother's eyes would get misty and she would say, "I was terribly homesick. I hated staying at the orphanage. Didn't I tell you, Frosula, that my life was like a novel? You have to write my story one day. I am not educated enough to write it myself."

Mother, despite the misery she felt inside, eventually adapted to her new environment and impressed the nuns with her scholastic ability and religious faith. She stayed at the orphanage until she was 14 years old. She liked studying and would have stayed longer, but the nuns started to exert pressure on her to convert from her Greek Orthodox faith to Catholicism. They wanted her to become a novice nun. Mother would laugh when she came to this part of her story and would say, "Yes, I was and still am a religious person, but I had no intention of becoming a nun. I wanted to marry and raise a family—the happy family that I never had as a child!"

When Mother left the orphanage at 14, (over Grandmother Eleni's objections), she lied about her age, and pretending to be 16 found a job as an assistant to a well-known tailor in Istanbul. She did well there and loved learning how to sew. She eventually became so accomplished at sewing that her boss would ask her to make her own patterns by cutting pieces on newspaper and transferring them onto cloth. She didn't earn a lot of money but made enough to take care of herself, and help her mother and brother as much as she could. She continued helping them all of her life despite feelings of resentment.

## Froso Hacipara Sendukas

I take another look at the wedding picture and get a lump in my throat. No wonder the young couple looks so happy. The two orphans had finally found a home in each other. I can only imagine all the hopes and aspirations that they brought to their marriage. Unfortunately they had no preparation or knowledge about "being married" and no healthy role models within their families.

According to my mother, their early married years were "not so bad." They didn't have much money and struggled to make ends meet. Mother took in sewing projects and Father was an apprentice to a professional photographer. Once he decided to go into his own photography business, Father converted an extra room in their apartment into a darkroom. As a young child, I was fascinated by the way Baba would take a blank film negative into the darkroom, immerse it in a tray filled with liquids, and pretty soon bring forth a picture with people's faces on it.

I saw the process as "magical" and would try to sneak into the darkroom as often as I could. Father would indulge me and let me stay with him for a while so long as I quickly closed the door behind me, not allowing light in.

Father did well right from the start, and after a while, Mother did not have to take on any more sewing projects. Her only sewing from then on would be to dress me, their only child, and herself. Father's special talent was "coloring" portraits and "re-touching." (In the '30s, in

## BRIDGING THE AEGEAN

Turkey, color photography was unavailable as it was quite new and very expensive.)

Soon word got around the Greek community of Istanbul about the young photographer who knew how to take flattering pictures at reasonable prices. In later years I recognized that he was a skilled natural salesman as well, especially with the ladies, both young and old. It didn't hurt that he was a good looking young man who smiled a lot.

By the time I started Greek elementary school Father was able to rent studio space in a very desirable location, Pera, in the heart of Istanbul's European district. In time his reputation grew even outside the Greek community. "Unfortunately," said Mother in retrospect, "the more successful Baba became within his profession, the less happy the marriage became." It seems that Father had a roving eye, and there were no shortages of women interested in flattering words even more than flattering pictures!

My own recollection of family life was that Baba was rarely home and, when he was, he and Mother would argue a lot. Mother would accuse Father of having affairs and he, in turn, would accuse her of being a super-jealous woman with a very active imagination. Oh, how I hated those arguments! Being an only child and the recipient of lots of affection from both of them, I didn't want to see them angry with each other. I would try to stop them by telling them not to yell at each other, and, when that didn't work, I would start crying. That would usually end the conflict. But there came a time when the arguments were more and more intense and I was powerless to stop them.

When I was 12 years old, my parents divorced. That was a big scandal in the Greek community, not only because divorce was rare but also because there were ugly rumors about infidelity. All of a sudden I was hesitant to even go for a walk on Pera or other prominent city streets. It felt like everybody was staring at me and whispering to each other about my family.

My mother took me aside one day to talk to me about the divorce. She must have seen my distress because she said, "Don't worry, Frosula, your father and I love you very much, and that will never change. He will always be your 'Baba.'" She was halfway right. I never doubted my parents' love—not once, not ever. But some things did change, some for the worse, some for the better.

Instead of one family, I now had to deal with two. Father quickly married the woman, Meri, whose name had been frequently mentioned in my parents' arguments, and within a few months Tula, a baby girl, was born. (At 12, I was pretty naïve, but even so, I understood why Baba had remarried so quickly after the divorce.)

I was no longer the only child in my father's world. That was, I admit, a hard pill to swallow. When the baby girl became a toddler and started following me around the house, I found Tula somewhat annoying, but also rather enjoyable.

My new stepmother was another story. I could never please the woman! She was very critical of me and she constantly complained about my behavior, manners and other things, even calling me a "spoiled brat" when my father was not present. Her pet peeve about me was that I had a habit of carrying a book everywhere I went. She would tell me that this was "rude behavior" and that I should stop doing it. I was shocked about her attitude, especially since my parents had never objected to my habit and even had encouraged me to love books. Thankfully, most of my time was spent at my familiar home—my mother's apartment. At least there I still had the status of beloved only child!

A year after the divorce my mother also remarried. But here's where I "lucked out." My new stepfather, John, was a nice surprise. He was an educated, cultured man who loved intelligent discussions about anything and everything. He was also a great storyteller, and dinnertime at home became an interesting adventure where I learned for the first time about the importance of having knowledge and opinions about world affairs.

Best of all was his personality. Unlike my father, he was an easy-going man who hated arguments and who got along with everybody, including me. He loved listening to all kinds of music—especially jazz—reading Ellery Queen mystery novels (my life-long love of mystery novels must have started then), and playing tavli (backgammon) with family members and friends. Our home became a much more peaceful habitat. Sure, I missed my father's presence, (I loved him dearly), but I did not miss the constant tension and arguments. Mother seemed a lot happier, and I was grateful for that too.

She and my stepfather stayed on good terms with my father—so much so that they eventually launched a successful business enterprise together (my stepfather was a photographer as well). When Mother's friends expressed astonishment at this turn of events, Mother would say, "I'm doing this primarily for Frosula's sake. She needs to see her parents as friends, not enemies."

Many years later, after my mother's death at age 67, I went back home for her memorial service and to empty the apartment of her belongings. After spending some time in Istanbul, her lifelong home, I completed taking care of her affairs and traveled to Athens, Greece to visit my father.

He came to pick me up at the Athens airport and hugged me. His eyes were misty. "I'm so sorry about your mother," he said, "I have been crying ever since I found out that she had died. I hope you know that there was a time when I loved her a lot. I still remember how I felt when we got married. She was so lovely in her wedding gown. I thought I was the luckiest man in the world. I wonder what happened to us and why on Earth we ever divorced!"

# BRIDGING THE AEGEAN

I looked at Baba with some astonishment and couldn't believe what my ears were hearing. Had he really forgotten all the endless arguments and yelling, along with his multiple affairs that went on during my growing up years?

As I listened to him talk about his version of the past, I finally understood that like me, he was also grieving—not just my mother's death but also the lost hopes of young Dimitri and Anastasia, the couple with stars in their eyes. I had seen that couple only once, in the small but treasured wedding picture I had found in Mother's belongings.

Nostalgia can lead to selective memory, I thought, but I didn't have the heart to contradict anything that my father was saying. I hugged him a little tighter and my tears mingled with his.

Froso Hacipara Sendukas

# BRIDGING THE AEGEAN

## MY MOTHER'S LOVE

I stayed in Athens for a week, and spent some quality time with Baba and my sister Tula. It was a touching and comforting week and I was very glad that I had come.

Even my stepmother, Meri—the nemesis of my youth—was decent, almost nice to me and before I left, gifted me with a vintage brooch that had been in her family for many years.

Baba and I spent most of our private time reminiscing about life with mother. I reminded him about a happy memory from when I was five or six years old that I had never forgotten.

"Do you remember the night of the puppets?" I asked. He shook his head "no," so I reminded him of that special night. "You and Mama came one evening to my bedside to tell me that you were going to the *Eliniko Siloyo* (Greek community center) to see a touring theatrical company from Greece. I was to stay home with our housekeeper. I wasn't too happy about that.

"If you remember, Baba, I loved plays and musicals, even at that young age. So I was disappointed that I had to go to sleep instead of going with you. Mama had told me that the play was for 'adults only,' so that was that. I pouted a little, but after a goodnight kiss from both of you, I fell asleep. The next thing I remember is my mother shaking me and trying to wake me up saying 'Frosula, get up. I need to dress you quickly and take you with me to the *Siloyo*. We don't have much time.'

"I was still half asleep and tried to understand what was going on. 'Where's Baba?' I asked. My mother replied that you were still at the theater and added, 'Don't ask any more questions. We have to go quickly so as to catch the rest of the show. They're having a long intermission. This is a wonderful show and I don't want you to miss it. Especially since a skit with puppets is coming on and I know how much you love puppets. Come, come, hurry up and dress! A taxi is waiting downstairs to take us back to the theater!' I must have fallen asleep again during the taxi ride because Mother was once again shaking me and saying, 'Frosula, wake up, honey, we're at the theater!' As we entered the building with Mother gently pushing me toward our seats, I saw you, Baba, standing up by your seat. I can still recall the look of shock on your face.

" 'I can't believe you did this!' I heard you telling Mother. 'You woke up our daughter from sound sleep and brought her here at 10:00 p.m. to see a musical? Anasto, have you lost your mind? The child is still half asleep!'

"That's when I realized that Mama had not told you about coming home during intermission to pick me up. I opened my eyes as wide as I could and I said, 'No, no, Baba, I'm not sleeping. I'm awake. Please don't be angry with Mama. I can't wait to see the puppets!' "

## BRIDGING THE AEGEAN

At that point in my re-telling, my father started laughing and said, "Yes, yes, now I remember. At first I was so angry with your mother for waking you up so late at night and bringing you to the theater, but then I saw the excitement in your eyes as you watched the puppets onstage and I got over my anger. I realized that your mother had acted out of love. You sat on my lap and tried so hard to stay awake that night, pethi mu!

"By the end of the musical you were in such deep sleep that I carried you in my arms to the car. You slept all the way home. As I put you to bed, you mumbled something about the puppets. You must have been dreaming about the play. No question about it, your mother loved you very much!"

I smiled through my tears. "You're so right, Baba," I said, 'that's why I have never forgotten that evening." Silently I added in my head, "Thank you Mama for all the love **and** for the extras like the puppets. You were always a Super Special Mom!"

I turned to my dad and said, "Did I ever tell you the story about the *pastirma?*"

I went on. "After I married and had children while living in the US, Mother made numerous trips to see me and my new family. On one of those trips, she asked my ex-husband and me what food we missed from home. Both of us told her the same thing—that we missed *pastirma,* (a processed meat made of beef that is used in Muslim countries as a substitute for forbidden pork.) With a little effort, we could scour Houston to find other familiar foods from our childhood, but not *pastirma*.

"We added, with emphasis, that it was strictly against the law to bring agricultural products, especially meat, into the US, and for Mother to not attempt to bring us *pastirma* **ever**. Telling Mama that she was not allowed to do something was like having a matador in a Spanish arena waving a red cloak in front of a bull while shouting 'Olé!'

"A year later, when Mother came from Istanbul to visit us again, she quickly told us that she had a nice surprise for us. She opened one of her suitcases and took out a package wrapped in foil. The package was wrapped beautifully, like a gift, with a big pink bow on top. As we unwrapped the 'mystery gift,' a big cylinder of *pastirma* rolled out of the package. It looked and smelled like the beloved meat we had known and missed for so long.

"We were flabbergasted. Mother looked triumphant. 'Mama!' I cried, "you broke the law in a very big way. Don't you remember we told you that travelers are not allowed to bring meat products from overseas? How on Earth did you get this through airport customs? Didn't anybody open and/or confiscate the package when they found out what it was?'

# BRIDGING THE AEGEAN

"Mother smiled and said, 'A customs agent *did* ask what was inside the foil gift package. I looked him straight in the eye and said, 'It's Turkish candy for my grandchildren.' The nice agent put the package back in my suitcase without opening it, smiled at me and told me to have a good time with my grandchildren. How about that?' "

My father started laughing and I joined him. Our mingled laughter lightened some of the heaviness in my heart I had felt ever since hearing of my mother's sudden death. Baba turned to me and said, "Only your mother would be determined enough and gutsy enough to get away with that kind of stunt. I sure hope you enjoyed your *pastirma.*"

"We sure did, Baba, we sure did!" I assured him.

In addition to sharing stories about my mother with Baba, I also had the opportunity following her memorial service in Istanbul to re-bond with my half sister Tula who I had not seen in several years. Tula told me that she had really liked my mother. She still vividly remembered the times she had spent in Mother's apartment. "Remember when I was five or six years old and you were babysitting me a few days? It was when my mother and Baba were out of town? And I ended up having surgery?" she reminisced.

I nodded my head. How could I ever forget **that** particular experience?

She went on. "I had a lump in my armpit and your mother said she didn't like the look of it. She asked me if my parents had taken me to a doctor, and I said 'No.' Next thing I knew your mother was taking me to her favorite surgeon, who removed it on the spot. Now I don't even have a scar. Well, Baba and Mother returned from the trip and I remember my mother became furious over what had happened. She told me that she would never again let me stay with you at your mother's apartment.

"Looking back, Froso, I think your mother did what she did out of caring for me, and I have always been grateful."

I thanked Tula for sharing her memory with me. I believed, as she did, that my mother's intentions were good and that she acted out of love. But I also remembered how awkward and scary that episode was for me. I was concerned about the lump, but I was also concerned about myself. At the time, I knew that Mother was overstepping her boundaries as she was prone to do and that there would be unpleasant consequences. My stepmother did not like me much anyway. This would give her another opportunity to be angry with me.

When I shared some of my concerns with Mama at the time, she shrugged and said, "This is all trivial compared to your sister's health. Baba and your stepmother are practicing 'careless neglect.' I have been watching the lump for some time now—it could be malignant for all we know. We'll let Dr. Violi decide what to do!"

# BRIDGING THE AEGEAN

Looking back, I cannot believe the surgeon agreed to do the procedure without Tula's parents' permission. In any event, my ever-resourceful mother managed to get it done. Who knows how she managed to convince him? And meanwhile, I was fretting that I would get in trouble for the unauthorized surgery.

That's exactly what happened. Upon her return, Meri saw her daughter's bandaged arm and started yelling at me, threatening that I would never babysit for my sister ever again. She refused to listen to my explanation and did not speak to me for a month. Now, listening to Tula's recollection of the event, I was happy she felt so positive about the experience.

Once again Mother's heart rather than her brain had dictated her actions and those of us who were in her path were swept along—mostly for the better!

Froso Hacipara Sendukas

## BRIDGING THE AEGEAN

### RETURN TO EPHESUS

In the fall of 2004, I embarked with close friends on a very special journey. We called it "Froso's back-to-her-roots journey." It combined sentiment and nostalgia with history and archaeology, and a very personal tour of two beautiful countries.

For years I kept promising to show my friends the country of my birth, Turkey, and the country of my native culture and ancestors, Greece. My friends gave me carte blanche in choosing the places we would visit. Since we only had two weeks at our disposal, it was vitally important to select favorite places and plan the trip accordingly.

I had no problem choosing where to go, I had always wanted to explore Turkey's Mediterranean coast. There was plenty of beauty there, mainly the luminous turquoise waters of the Aegean Sea. I was also eager to see the wonderful Greco-Roman historical ruins of the area, dating back to the Byzantine Empire. I knew that in the last fifty years there had been numerous archaeological excavations in the area, yielding some wonderful finds pertaining to ancient Greek civilizations.

I was especially keen on going to Ephesus, a site that had been, in its heyday, an important learning center, with a famous library that had been named one of the seven wonders of the ancient world. Ephesus had also been considered a sacred site because of the cult of the goddess Artemis.

# Froso Hacipara Sendukas

Because of its proximity to Izmir (or "Smyrna" as the city was called by the Byzantine Greeks—a lovely city by any name, and an important seaside port), Ephesus was also a vibrant market place famous for silk textiles and exotic spices brought by ships from all over the world, especially from Arabia.

My interest in Ephesus was based on much more than its historical importance. I had been to Ephesus almost fifty years earlier during a college trip in the spring of 1955.

At the time, I was a junior at the American College for Girls, a private school in Istanbul. Our school had leased a train to take our class as well as two teachers on a tour of the Mediterranean coast of Turkey.

During the trip we saw some wonderful examples of Greco-Roman civilization. International teams of archaeologists were just beginning to work in the area to excavate some important historical finds and ancient treasures.

One of these teams was hard at work in Ephesus when we arrived to tour the site. The archaeological area was off limits to visitors. All we could observe from some distance was a lot of buckets, a dirt trail and people in animated conversation in diverse languages.

Not that my classmates and I cared that much about the archaeological work going on around us. I remember discussing at length whether in a few days we would be allowed to swim in the beautiful, natural pools of Pamukkale, an amazing site close to Ephesus, famous for its all white, spectacular lime cascades formed by the hot springs of the area. It was the most beautiful natural phenomenon I had ever seen! From a distance it looked like a hill made out of cotton, so the Turks called it Pamukkale (a hill of cotton).

I still have a picture of a young me in a bathing suit, with two classmates by my side, standing in a small, spring-fed pool with a big smile on my face. I must have just experienced the lovely sensation of the warm water, hence the big smile.

On our last day at Ephesus, we were eating lunch when we heard a lot of shouting. It seemed to come from the site of the archaeological dig. We ran to see what was causing the sudden excitement. We were not allowed to get too close to the activity, but when the archaeologist who was in charge of the project found out that we were college students and spoke English, he sent one of the volunteers to come and talk to us. He told us that they had just dug out of the ground the head of a statue. Some of the archaeologists in the group believed that the head belonged to a statue of the goddess Artemis. The person telling us all this was so excited that he could hardly speak.

He also told us that he and the rest of the group had been at Ephesus for some months now. During that time, they had excavated many Greco-Roman coins and some other relics, but today's discovery was by far the most important. It made the whole volunteer experience worthwhile, he said.

After the young man went back to the dig, one of our teachers was quick to point out how lucky we were to witness, even from a distance, such an important historical find.

I remember feeling a touch of pride that all these archaeologists (and many more to come through the following years), had traveled from far away and worked so hard to find symbols and links to my Greek-Roman ancestors! Being part of the minority Christian population in Turkey and thus not enjoying political clout or status, it felt good to relish, even for a few minutes, that my roots went all the way back to the culture-rich Greek civilizations that flourished in the area thousands of years ago!

Looking at the archaeological site I could only see a small part of the excavation, but I wondered at the time what the rest of the statue looked like and what else was buried in the fertile ground of Ephesus.

I left Turkey in 1956, and throughout all the years of living in the US and raising a family, I always dreamed of going back to Ephesus and seeing the results of many years of archaeological exploration.

Once, leafing through a National Geographic magazine, I saw an article on excavations in Turkey. It mentioned Ephesus as being one of the best

# BRIDGING THE AEGEAN

examples of international archaeological teamwork and the wonderful discovery of ancient treasures! There were some pictures with the article, and I was thrilled to see that the whole exterior of the famous Celsus Library had been excavated, and there was even a statue of a goddess in one of its arches.

Immediately my mind flashed back to the college trip of my youth and how I was witness to the digging out of the head of statue of a goddess.

I was moved by the article and the pictures and wondered if this was the same statue that I had seen in 1955! I decided that it didn't really matter. That issue of the National Geographic magazine reinforced my desire to return to Ephesus one day and see for myself the changes that had occurred.

Even though I had gone back to Turkey several times through the years, the trips consisted mostly of visiting my mother, who lived in Istanbul. After my mother died in 1981, I had not gone back to Turkey. I could not bear the thought of arriving in Yeşilköy at the Istanbul airport and not having her welcome me.

So, when my friends asked me to organize a personal tour to Turkey and Greece, it gave me the opportunity not only to return to my birthplace, which I had missed, but also to retrace some of the steps of my youthful trip of 1955.

## Froso Hacipara Sendukas

Naturally, Ephesus was at the top of my list. Selecting the rest was not so easy. Travel has always been much more than a hobby for me—passion is more like it. I have visited many countries and places through the years, especially after my children were grown, and loved the whole experience, even when the trips were not perfect. So I loved the idea of arranging a travel tour to places I knew and loved. However, I soon found out that arranging a tour for three was a very different endeavor from just going on a tour. After a couple of time-consuming and frustrating months, I gave up the idea of doing it all by myself and asked a travel agent to help me. Later, I was very glad that I did.

I decided that we did not need a driver for Istanbul. After all, the city is relatively easy to navigate with buses, trains, a tunnel and inexpensive taxis. Even though it has the reputation of being exotic and mysterious, to me it's just my lovely birthplace! Since I spent the first 22 years of my life there, my pride would not allow hiring a stranger to show us the sights.

I did, however, ask the agent to hire a local driver for the Mediterranean coast, (due to limited public transportation and great distances between ruins), but no tour guide or translator. I had promised my friends to be their personal tour guide, and I wanted to keep my promise. After all, I spoke both Greek and Turkish. I was not fluent in the languages anymore, but still able to understand people and to be understood. This turned out to be a humbling experience. After a week or so of constantly translating three languages, I came to appreciate tour guides a lot more!

We first met Mahmut, our driver, when we arrived in Izmir. He was at the airport, holding a sign with our misspelled names. I introduced myself and my companions and he was duly impressed by my knowledge of the Turkish language. Mahmut knew about three words of English. He told me that he usually worked in tandem with local guides and was surprised that I had not wanted any.

The van he met us with was a late model Mercedes Benz, and we had plenty of space to ourselves. It had seating for 10–12 people.

Since our trip was planned and achieved with a limited budget, I was surprised to see the luxury van. However, since we had already paid for the tour, I decided to go with the flow and not to worry. The hotel that Mahmut drove us to was also very nice; it had four stars so I silently blessed my travel agent.

I was so excited about going to Ephesus the next day that I slept fitfully that night, dreaming of Byzantine relics. At last morning arrived and we went to the hotel dining room for breakfast. As I entered the room I saw that our driver was already there having his own breakfast.

At precisely 9:00 a.m. (our prearranged time of departure) we piled into the van and Mahmut drove us to the place that I had dreamed about so many timed during my busy American life. Ephesus had always been in the periphery of my memory, beckoning me to return.

Mahmut stopped the van after a while and said in the few English words that he knew, "Welcome! This is Ephesus."

I looked around in amazement. We seemed to be in the middle of nowhere. All I saw around me was a dirt road and a metal gate. What I was seeing was so different from what was embedded in my memory that I seriously thought that Mahmut had made a mistake and had taken us to the wrong place.

I asked him if this was really Ephesus. He pointed to a small ticket window, half-hidden by a gigantic tree. There were two words written on top—"Ephesus" and "Efes" (the Turkish word for Ephesus). I bought us three tickets and hesitantly walked to the closed gate.

As I walked closer to the gate, I was able to see some classical Greek columns behind the gate, and my heart leaped with joyful anticipation.

Once we were inside the gate, the dirt road disappeared and we seemed to be in a different world. A small sign told us in English and Turkish that the excavated cobblestone and marble streets we were walking on dated from the 1st century A.D.

# BRIDGING THE AEGEAN

Our path was lined with Ionian and Ionic style columns of varied sizes. The contrast between the view outside the main gate of Ephesus and the view inside was so extreme that it reminded me of a movie that I had seen as a child, I believe that it was called Ali Baba and the Forty Thieves. One scene that I still remember vividly showed a gate in the middle of an arid looking desert, and inside the gate were the spoils of the thieves. There were chests everywhere overflowing with gold artifacts, chains and sparkling jewels!

Ephesus was not quite like the movie. There were no chests lying around full of gold, but as we walked around we did see many fragments of what looked like broken pieces of statues and relics. We even saw the headless torso of a Greco-Roman statue of a soldier made out of marble. Even without a head he looked ready to go to battle!

I was astounded to see this amazing relic lying on the ground behind the classical columns. There were also some chests with inscriptions on them almost casually strewn around.

I seriously thought that those objects belonged in a museum, or in some other protected area. The more we saw of these ancient treasures the more upset I became. I felt some anger towards the governmental authorities who were in charge of safeguarding historical sites. What were they thinking?

I may not have been fair, but I even thought that perhaps some politics may have been involved. Given the long history of feuding between

Turkey and Greece I wondered if the attitude of authority figures would have been any different if the site yielded relics pertaining to Ottoman or Turkish history instead of ancient Greek history.

In addition to the headless torso of the soldier, there were various animals sculpted on ceramic, stone and even on marble. Most of them had parts missing—an ear, or a nose or other parts of their bodies, but even so I wondered once again why those precious finds, thousands of years old, were not protected from the elements as well as human hands. Since I commented aloud this time my friend Connie overhead me and reminded me that these relics had already survived thousands of years and surely could survive a few a more. I laughed, but I was not totally convinced.

There were no signs telling us not to touch the historical relics. I looked for one, in vain. There was one small sign telling visitors not to take anything from the site and that was all.

I also noticed that there was not a single guard on the premises. I felt a strong, crazy urge to gather up all these relics that symbolized a flourishing and now dead ancient civilization and protect them somehow!

I watched a few tourists walk by, seemingly unimpressed about walking on marble streets and being surrounded by all these treasures. I wanted to shout out to them "Do you realize where you are and what amazing objects you are seeing? Do you know that St. Paul walked on some of the same streets that we're walking on?"

My friends, seeing me lost in thought, did not ask many questions. One of them did approach me and asked if I could read and translate the inscription on a marble chest. I saw that it was written in ancient Greek, and warned them not to have too many expectations. I explained that there were substantial differences between the ancient and modern Greek languages. I tried to read the inscription anyway. I was surprised and rather thrilled to discover that I could read and understand most of the words on the chest.

It talked about the importance of "fairness" and "justice" in governing a "polis" (city/state). For the first time I understood that the much maligned word "politics" came from the Greek word "polis" and originally referred to the noble governing of a city. I was so excited that I was able to understand and translate most of the writing on the chest, that I immediately took a picture of the relic!

Later we visited the official museum in Ephesus. When I saw its marble floors (excavated from the site) and how it was packed to the gills with ancient Greco-Roman treasures, I understood a little better why so many historical relics were left on the ground. There definitely was an abundance of riches here. There were wall to wall statues everywhere.

## Froso Hacipara Sendukas

Ephesus was an important city in the 1st century A.D., sort of a combination of New York and Las Vegas. It had a sacred mission as well—two missions to be exact. It was originally a symbol of the cult of Artemis, an important goddess of Greek mythology. Artemis was worshipped here as a "protector" of the city, and pilgrims came from all over the Roman Empire to celebrate during the annual festivities given in her honor.

Much later Ephesus would be known in theological circles as the place where the apostle Paul came after the crucifixion and resurrection of Jesus to spread the new gospel and form a new religion—Christianity.
I do not know what exactly brought Paul to Ephesus. Maybe it was the challenge that the town represented. In addition to being famous as a learning center, Ephesus had the reputation of being a town where visitors and/or pilgrims could have a whale of a good time, especially during the festivities honoring Artemis.

The temple of Artemis was an impressive edifice with lots of imposing columns. Ephesians took pride in the fact that their temple was bigger and more famous than the Parthenon of Athens, Greece. In fact, it was at one time considered to be one of the seven wonders of the ancient world!

Unfortunately, it has not survived for posterity. A fire burned it to the ground, and very little of it survived. Archaeological excavations through the years discovered only one column of the temple.

# BRIDGING THE AEGEAN

Ephesus must have truly been a pretty town. It had public baths of some renown and a big gymnasium (ancient Greeks believed that a fit mind needed to reside in a fit body!). There were decorative fountains adorning many parts of the city, and of course we cannot forget the famous Celsus Library that rivaled the one in Alexandria, Egypt.

This is the town that Paul chose to spread the gospel of his teacher, Jesus. You have to admire the gumption of the man! Here he was addressing crowds in a city where many of its residents made their living by supporting a cult to a heathen goddess. He was telling them—or rather preaching to them—to stop worshipping a multitude of gods and goddesses and instead accept that there was only one God who sent his only son to Earth in the form of a man—a lowly carpenter by trade—to save mankind!

Paul must have also talked of witnessing healings and miracles and all the wise lessons that Jesus taught through stories and parables. And, of course, how he was crucified and then resurrected, to join his Heavenly Father.

As if this amazing story wasn't enough, Paul asked the crowds to repent their sins and turn away from the city's lewd activities. He wanted them to become pure in thought and behavior so that one day they could join Jesus in Heaven and attain eternal life (after their physical death that is).

## Froso Hacipara Sendukas

The above message must have been a hard sell in Ephesus, especially early on. Here was this Roman stranger attacking their religion, their lifestyle, their morals and even their commerce! I can imagine him in the front amphitheater trying to convert minds and hearts while the residents, boisterous and loud as Greeks tend to be, were probably laughing at him and his crazy ideas. Frankly, I think he was lucky not to have been stoned by the crowds!

Both ancient and modern Greeks love drama and heated, intense debates about anything and everything. One piece of evidence of the above is the multitude of open-air theaters on all the historical sites that we visited.

Fortunately for Paul, Greeks are also impressed by oratory eloquence and courage. By all accounts of his time Paul was an impressive and effective speaker. He was also a man who believed in his mission and was tenacious and persistent despite formidable opposition. That must have impressed the Greeks of Ephesus. How could it not? So after a while, the crowds must have stopped laughing or jeering at him and started paying more attention to his message. Pretty soon, he was having some success in his attempts to convert the populace.

Many theologians believe that the foundation of Christianity was laid by Paul in Ephesus around 50 A.D. I was thinking of Paul and his time in Ephesus as I was walking with my friends. We were following a sign that was taking us to the library. Suddenly there I was, standing in front of the façade of the building, and I was mesmerized. How beautiful it was! There were two arches built on each side of the exterior and the statues of two regal goddesses in flowing robes standing in their rightful places inside those arches.

"How lovely the goddesses look," I thought and wondered if either one of them had been excavated 49 years ago, during my first visit to Ephesus. I realized that I did not really want to know the answer to my question. What I did know was that I was a young girl of 21 when I saw the head of a goddess emerge from the ground, and here I was at age 70, a mother of three and a grandmother of seven, admiring the completed work. The thought made me choke with emotion, and I burst into tears.

I stood in front of the library for a long time, breathing the fresh, unpolluted air and watching the pretty yellow wild flowers that framed the library sway to the afternoon breeze. It was such a lovely view that I did not want it leave it, then or ever!

I imagined how the complete library must have looked thousands of years ago, with scholars in long, loose clothes arriving from all parts of the Roman Empire and engaging in animated conversations in ancient Greek or Latin or even Aramaic.

My companions, who had seen me lost in nostalgia and sentiment, came by to remind me that there were more historical sites to see before the place closed for the day. I heard their logic and tore myself away from the wonderful library. I left it physically, but it has never left me!

Before leaving the area, we visited the house where the Virgin Mary is thought to have spent the last years of her life. The house is situated above the Ephesus ruins on top of a hill. The view was so spectacular! The house is called "Meryem Ana Evi" in Turkish. Loosely translated it means the "House of the Holy Mother." There was a large tree in the front of the tiny house. It provided shade and looked to be very old indeed.

There was something strange about the tree. The branches looked almost white (instead of green) because of the hundreds of pieces of paper that were tacked to the tree. We did not know what the papers were until we went inside the house. There was an official-looking plaque inside the house, saying that a certain Pope (I don't remember which one) had visited the house and had declared it to be Mary's authentic house where she lived her last years,

What caught my attention inside the house was a wall covered with folded pieces of paper, just like the ones covering the branches of the tree outside the house. A guide at the house told us that this was the "gratitude wall" where visitors left notes and letters thanking Mother Mary. I was startled to see that many of these notes were written in Turkish. They were thanking the Mother of Jesus for helping them become mothers themselves.

# BRIDGING THE AEGEAN

As I was trying to figure out how the mostly Muslim women came to write the thank you notes, a Turkish tour guide going by with a tourist group explained to them that "Meryem Ana" had a reputation in Turkey for helping infertile women become fertile and have children! "Many Turkish women believe this," he said, "and even though they are devout Muslims in their religion and faith, they still pray to the Christian Mother Mary!" He added, "The success rate is high, but they often keep these prayers and beliefs secret even in their own families, hence the many anonymous thank you notes!

Even though I was born in Turkey and spent my youth there, the tour guide's message was a total surprise. I was touched by what I heard. "How wonderful," I thought, "that occasionally faith can transcend formal religions!"

The visit to Mary's house concluded our time at Ephesus. I had a very hard time leaving the place. I wanted to stay there a lot longer than I had planned. However, we had a deadline, and I had been the one who had set it up. We were to meet Mahmut, our private chauffeur, the next morning, and he was to take us to other historical ruins/sites along Turkey's Mediterranean coast to view some more wonderful examples of the Greco-Roman, Byzantine civilizations that had flourished in the area for centuries.

I definitely was looking forward to visiting the remaining sites. Some of these would be new places for me as well. And yet, my reaction to

Froso Hacipara Sendukas

Ephesus on this return trip was so emotional and so intense that if our trip had ended right there and then, I would have been totally fine and totally satisfied that I had been on a wonderful and magical journey!

# BRIDGING THE AEGEAN

## AN UNPLEASANT ENCOUNTER IN MARMARIS

The return trip to Turkey had been wonderful up til now. Even a bout with high blood pressure in the beginning of the trip that resulted in an unexpected visit to a hospital emergency room turned out fine. I was treated swiftly and inexpensively by a Turkish doctor, and I had been impressed by his knowledge and empathy.

Any trepidation I may have felt early on in the momentous journey as to how I would be treated as a Greek had mostly vanished. I can truthfully say that I had not detected any hostility or prejudice against me.

Whenever I spoke Turkish, the typical local reaction was pleasant surprise, and nothing else.

It was only when we arrived in Marmaris on our 12th day in Turkey and the last leg of our Turkish journey, that I realized despite the joy of being back "home," the wonder of the marvelous Byzantine ruins, and the beauty of the Mediterranean region, I had been carrying some emotional baggage. Now I could finally exhale and just be a happy tourist—or so I thought.

It seems that I exhaled just a little too soon. As we entered the hotel that my travel agent had chosen for us, I did my usual routine of approaching the desk to confirm our reservations and register our group of three persons. As I did this, (in Turkish as usual), the hotel manager, behind the desk, immediately asked if I was a professional tour guide. When I said, "No, I am not a tour guide," he then asked me how did I know the language. "Very few tourists know Turkish," he said.

By now, after registering in numerous hotels in the country, I was used to this kind of inquiry. I smiled and gave him my usual explanation that I had been born in Istanbul many years ago, and thus still spoke passable Turkish. I was stunned by his reaction. Instead of accepting my explanation, he told me in a hostile tone that he did not believe me. "Is this some kind of joke?" he said. "Why are you fabricating untrue stories about your birth? Are you making fun of me?"

I was so shocked by his rude and hostile remarks that I was speechless.

Overhearing all of this, and seeing my reaction, another man behind the desk approached the hotel manager and said, "It's your name that puzzles us. It's obviously not a Turkish name and that's the reason probably that our manager said what he said. I don't understand your explanation, either. How could this happen in our country?"

I finally found my voice. I looked at both men and said "I guess you two are too young to remember this, but fifty years ago, when I was growing up there were 100,000 Greeks who lived here and were Turkish citizens. They all had Greek names, just like me! Now can I have the keys to our rooms, please?"

# BRIDGING THE AEGEAN

As I said in the above words, I tried to keep my voice calm, but my insides were churning with emotion. The hostile words flung at me at the hotel lobby instantly brought back some unpleasant ghosts of the past, and I found myself shaking with shock and distress.

On the surface I was the same 70-year-old woman, mother, grandmother and licensed psychotherapist who had entered the hotel ten minutes ago, but inside I had been transformed into my 12-year-old self, on a bus somewhere (anywhere), in Istanbul, wearing a pendant in the shape of a cross (having momentarily forgotten her mother's warnings) and hearing the word gâvur (infidel) loudly whispered by a couple of older men as they approached my bus seat. The carefree 12-year-old, shattered by the words, feeling very small and very vulnerable.

I turned my back to the manager and to his assistant so they wouldn't see that my eyes were stinging with tears.

As I approached my friends waiting for me at the lobby, Connie must have seen a strange expression on my face, because she quickly said, "Is something wrong, Froso, did we come to the wrong hotel or something? You look pale and upset."

I realized since they did not speak nor understand Turkish, that they had no idea of the drama that had taken place a few yards from where they stood. "Unfortunately we came to the right hotel," I said, "at least the one listed in our travel plan. Let's go to our rooms and I'll tell you what happened."

After they heard what had transpired, both of my friends were indignant about the way I was treated and asked me if I wanted to leave and go someplace else.

Perhaps we should have left. But, I tried to be practical and logical and reminded them that we had already paid for our accommodations and that we were leaving in the morning to go to a Greek island. I told them I was OK with staying. Later, I gave myself a self-talk. The trip so far had been great despite some apprehension on my part when we started. I told myself I should not allow one bad apple, namely the hotel manager, to spoil the positive experience of the last 12 days in Turkey.

Despite the sensible talk, and my friends' comforting presence, my sleep was very restless that night, with numerous nightmares. I felt the ghosts of the past were not ready to leave me as yet.

# BRIDGING THE AEGEAN

## TAKING THE FERRY FROM TURKEY TO GREECE

If you look at a map of the Mediterranean region, it's easy to see how close—geographically speaking—the countries of Turkey and Greece are to one another. In fact, some Greek islands are closer to Turkey than their own country.

An example of this is the island of Mitilini where my paternal grandfather, Panayiotis Hadjiparas, was born.

Despite this physical proximity, it often seemed as if there was a wide chasm between the two countries.

I know that feuds and tensions between neighboring countries are not rare. World history is full of territorial conflicts and bloody wars that have lasted for hundreds of years and animosities that never totally go away.

As the daughter of two Greek parents, with language, culture, and religion different from the majority of Turkish citizens, I knew from personal experience about feuds, chronic enmity, and the emotional damage that often results from the above.

It is ironic but true that only after emigrating to the US could I enjoy a close and meaningful friendship with Turkish-born friends who happened to be Muslim rather than Christian/Greek Orthodox like me. Away from our native soil and families of origin, we quickly found out that we had more similarities than differences. Like other homesick immigrants from all over the world, we were united by nostalgia for our beautiful birthplace and comforted each other by reminiscing about our past while sharing our new present. While sharing stories about opportunities in the host country, we would also share some confusion about cultural differences and turn to each other for support when facing the unfamiliar. We marinated the meats we found in American supermarkets with olive oil, oregano and yogurt and placed them on skewers to make them taste more Middle Eastern and familiar. (In the early days in Alexandria Louisiana, I often had to go to health food stores to find yogurt and at times even olive oil as well!)

As the days in the new country turned into weeks, and months, and years, we started skewering the Turkish language as well, and more and more English words entered our conversational mix. We would repeat the same jokes over and over again and still enjoy them. We would quote old Turkish proverbs to each other. When we couldn't remember all the words, we would add our own embellishments.

For years we laughed at the true story of a member of our expatriate group who, while trying to arrange a wedding, called a local judge and asked "Judge, will you marry me?" The answer came quickly, "No, I will not marry you, but I'll be happy to perform a wedding ceremony!" Kind of a corny joke perhaps, but it still produced laughter.

# BRIDGING THE AEGEAN

We shared similar stories about our linguistic faux pas, laughing at ourselves, but with no malice whatsoever. Once again, the warm cocoon of friendship made the immigrant experience less painful and much more tolerable. How sad it would have been to miss this loving friendship of many years because of differences of religion or ethnic origin!

As I was reading the above reflections to my son, Ronny, and his wife Lisa, my son spoke up, "Mom," he said, "I was only a young boy at the time, but I still remember how excited you and Dad would get every time your Turkish friends visited us or when we would go to visit them, especially during the holidays. Even in the years when we lived in Baltimore, Maryland and they were in Louisiana. As the calendar moved to the middle of December, we kids always hoped that we would get together with them. Somehow the holidays were different, much more festive and joyful when the two or three families of your former group had a reunion. You and Dad looked so much happier when you were with them. You would start talking non-stop, mostly in Turkish, and even though we didn't understand what you were saying, it was really nice to see you guys smiling and laughing.

"You didn't pay that much attention to us kids, but even that was OK. Since we didn't grow up with grandparents, cousins, etc., these reunion visits were for us the closest thing to being with a warm, extended family. Plus, they were always so nice to us!"

I was touched by my son's recollection and was happy that he shared it with me. I always knew that these friendships played a unique and valuable role in my own life, but I had not realized how important it had been to my children as well.

Often through the years, I have thought of the special bond that my son was talking about, and wondered...if diverse individuals can connect and love each other through the years, why can't neighbor countries be friendly and enjoy their similarities, instead of harping about differences? Wouldn't a friendly détente be to their mutual advantage? Maybe I'm being naïve and unrealistic, but that doesn't stop me from wishing it.

While planning the 2004 trip to my native land, the subject of "friendship" and "cooperation" between countries was very much on my mind. I knew that many years of feuding about territorial and political issues (especially Cyprus) had made "peaceful co-existence", let alone, "friendship" a very difficult proposition for Greece and Turkey.

I remembered, during my growing-up years how fearful I would be every time I heard any negative news involving the two countries. I knew from personal experience (e.g., the Turkish-Greek riots in Istanbul in 1955) that it is often the members of a minority population that pay the price for political conflict, and I would get fearful about planning such a trip.

# BRIDGING THE AEGEAN

However, I reminded myself that in recent years I had seen a hopeful development, thanks to the popularity of travel to the Mediterranean region, especially by cruise ship. Looking at the itineraries of cruise lines to the area, I saw that more and more touring companies were offering travel packages that included both Greece and Turkey.

Tourists didn't seem to care about century-old divisions and/or territorial and religious feuds. They wanted to relax and enjoy beautiful, natural vistas as well as fascinating ruins of extinct empires and civilizations. The two countries closest to my heart had plenty of both. The shimmering turquoise and azure-blue waters of the Aegean and the Mediterranean seas beckoned as well, regardless which country's national flag was flying overhead.

The languages were different, but the food was very similar and tasty, and according to numerous nutritional studies, healthy as well. It wasn't lost on travelers that many natives of both countries live to a ripe old age!

As I was arranging the "return to my roots" trip, I wondered if relations between the two neighbors (and ex-enemies) had improved enough that we could travel directly from Marmara (in southern Turkey) to Rhodes, a famous Greek island, that I always wanted to visit.

Again, looking at the familiar map of the region, I could see that the two places were quite close. Could we even go by ferryboat, I wondered? I had always loved ferryboats. One of my most cherished memories of growing up in Turkey was taking the ferryboat every summer to commute between Burgaz (the island where my family spent most summers) and Istanbul. Since no cars were allowed in the Prince Islands there were no cars on the boat, just people, (mostly men) commuting back and forth on a daily basis between their jobs in the mainland and the three islands where their families spent the summer.

On weekends the picture changed somewhat. The commuters were mostly whole families who couldn't afford or did not want to rent cottages for the season and who would go either to visit families/friends or to enjoy sunning and swimming and/or having a picnic in one of the islands just for the day or for the weekend.

As a child, I used to beg my mother to join the commuters occasionally and take me along, so I could ride on the Istanbul-Burgaz ferryboat. My favorite place to sit was the upper decks, especially during sunset. I would marvel at how the lovely strips of color on the horizon changed and varied with each sunset, and how the Sea of Marmara glowed after each sunset. I would take deep breaths, taking in the smell of the sea, and delighting in the sensation of the gentle Aegean/Mediterranean breezes playing with my hair!

Unfortunately, most of the time my mother preferred to sit inside, in the covered part of the ferry. Being a protective mother, she would not let me go outside to sit by myself, at least, not till I became a teenager.

# BRIDGING THE AEGEAN

My consolation inside was the ever present non-alcoholic bar, filled with a great variety of local fruit juices, hot tea, and Turkish coffee. My favorite drink (before I discovered that I liked the expertly-made foamy coffee) was g*azoz* (similar to 7-Up).

I'm aware that nostalgia can alter and embellish our memorable moments, so it's possible that the boat rides may not have all been as wonderful as I remember them. My basic belief about this is that the full authenticity of memories does not really matter that much, just as long as we are as truthful as we can be with the facts that are embedded in our minds as well as our hearts. After all, I know as a psychotherapist that it's not events themselves that thrill us or traumatize us—it's how we interpret these events!

Since I have nothing but happy memories about ferryboats, I think it's easy to understand why the idea of going from Turkey to Greece via ferry was so appealing to me!

According to the travel books I consulted, this kind of trip was currently possible, but I was still not totally trusting what I read. I knew from personal experience that politics could quickly get in the way, and tensions between the two countries could flare up in the blink of an eye, ruining any and all travel plans. At the risk of being called paranoid, I have to confess that I decided to call the Turkish consulate in Houston, where I live, and ask them directly if such a travel plan was possible.

## Froso Hacipara Sendukas

I was a little apprehensive doing this and suspect that here again, my past as a member of a minority (at times, a harassed minority) played a big role in making me wary of dealing with authority figures, especially those that represented the "old country." I even debated with myself- while feeling a little foolish doing so about what language to use when calling. I settled on English, thinking it was more neutral.

I was thrilled to find out from the call that the contemporary travel books were right and that yes we could travel from Marmara, Turkey, to Rhodes, Greece by ferryboat. All we had to do was obtain a temporary Greek visa in Marmara and then buy a ticket for a daily boat going to Rhodes.

And that's exactly what we did! The weather on the day of our ferryboat adventure was perfect. It was sunny and warm without a cloud in the sky. I saw this as a good sign. When I woke up in the morning, despite all the assurances that had been given to me, I still felt anxiety that something could still go wrong. As I dressed I made sure that I wore my *mavi goz* (blue eye) bracelet, to protect me against any evil envy that might be coming my way! After all, I grew up in two cultures that strongly believed in this centuries-old superstition. Just judging by the hundreds of souvenirs in many, many forms that are widely available in the street and flea markets of both Greece and Turkey, it is easy to see how strongly the belief (and commerce of it) is embedded in both cultures.

# BRIDGING THE AEGEAN

As a child, I remember laughing at the idea that wearing a certain object could keep people from harm. When I told my mother of my doubts, she gently scolded me and told me to not ever laugh at people's beliefs. Even the Old Testament in the Bible mentions *to mati* (the eye) she said. Being the kind of person she was she didn't want to believe that people could be evil, so her interpretations of "the evil eye" superstition went something like this. "It's not that people are evil, Frosula," she would say, "or intentionally want to harm us, but sometimes they may innocently envy something we own, and their thoughts can affect us in a negative way. Do you understand, Frosula?" I understood.

So, some 50 years later, standing in the hotel room and getting dressed for the "big adventure", I made sure that I was armed with my special "blue eye" bracelet against any and all, intentional or unintentional envy of any and all passersby.

I was excited and nervous at the same time. I led my small travel group to Marmara's docks. I am not an early riser, but I made sure that we were there by 7:30 a.m.

Upon arriving at the designated place, I saw that a waiting line had already formed in front of the closed window of a small white building. There was a sign at the window that said—in Turkish and English—that this was the place to obtain temporary visas to Greece, starting at 8:00 a.m. At another window nearby another sign proclaimed that this was the place to buy tickets for the boat trip to Rhodes. The first boat of the day was scheduled to leave at 8:30 a.m.

What a relief it was to see those signs. I finally relaxed realizing that my long standing dream was about to become reality. My two companions stood in line calmly, unaware of the emotional drama taking place inside me. I read somewhere that the place where a person is born "marks" him/her forever. I thought of that sentence throughout the trip, but especially that October morning in 2004, standing at the docks in Marmara!

My two ethnic identities were finally working as a team on this day, happily linking the two countries of my roots, instead of pulling me back and forth and causing me distress.

Wonderful as the whole trip was, nothing could equal my intense emotions as—ticket in hand—I set foot on the boat taking us to Rhodes. I was thrilled to speak Turkish as I entered the ferryboat, leaving beautiful Marmara behind, and equally thrilled to speak Greek as I left the boat to set foot on the lovely island of Rhodes.

I cried, both times, but these were tears of joy.